Mini Delights

Mini Delights

Tiny but perfect cakes, pies, desserts, & sweets

First published by Parragon Books Ltd in 2013
LOVE FOOD is an imprint of Parragon Books Ltd

Parragon Inc.
440 Park Avenue South, 13th Floor
New York, NY 10016
www.parragon.com/lovefood

ISBN: 978-1-4723-2350-7

Printed in China

Created and produced by Pene Parker and Rebecca Spry
Cakes: author and home economist Joanna Farrow; photographer Noel Murphy
Pies: author and home economist Sara Lewis; photographer Stephen Conroy
Desserts: author and home economist Sara Lewis; photographer William Shaw
Sweets: author and home economist Sunil Vijayakar; photographer Karen Thomas

Notes for the Reader

This book uses standard kitchen measuring spoons and cups. All spoon and cup measurements
are level unless otherwise indicated. Unless otherwise stated, milk is assumed to be whole, eggs
are large, individual vegetables are medium, and pepper is freshly ground black pepper. Unless
otherwise stated, all root vegetables should be washed in plain water and peeled prior to using.

Garnishes, decorations, and serving suggestions are all optional and not necessarily included in
the recipe ingredients or method.

The times given are only an approximate guide. Preparation times differ according to the
techniques used by different people and the cooking times may also vary from those given.
Optional ingredients, variations, or serving suggestions have not been included in the time
calculations.

Recipes using raw or very lightly cooked eggs should be avoided by infants, the elderly, pregnant
women, convalescents, and anyone with a weakened immune system. Pregnant and breast-feeding
women are advised to avoid eating peanuts and peanut products. People with nut allergies should
be aware that some of the prepared ingredients used in the recipes in this book may contain nuts.
Always check the packaging before use.

Contents

Introduction

Tiny portions of our favorite treats are fun to make and so easy to eat. They look cute and, because they are only bite-size morsels, they make the perfect finish for a special dinner, an informal get-together, or a celebration party. The cakes include everything from delicious fruit loaves to miniature wedding cakes. Bite-size pies made with delicious buttery pastry will melt in your mouth and are surprisingly easy to make. Impress your friends at your next dinner party by serving two or three different mini desserts on one plate, like in a trendy restaurant, or round off your meal with a selection of homemade sweets that look terrific and won't leave you feeling guilty.

Ingredients

Eggs

Eggs are basic ingredients in baking. They serve many functions, providing structure, color, texture, flavor, and moisture. Always check the dates on the carton, use eggs that are fresh, and store them in the refrigerator. Do not use egg substitutes in place of fresh eggs.

Flour

All-purpose flour is used in this book. It has a medium gluten content. It can be white or whole-wheat and does not contain a leavening agent. Don't substitute whole-wheat flour for white all-purpose flour in these recipes because it is heavier and more dense, so it will change the texture of the recipe. Self-rising flour has baking powder and salt added, so don't use it as a substitute for all-purpose flour unless the recipe includes baking powder and salt and you make adjustments. As a guide, 1 cup of self-rising flour has 1½ teaspoons of baking powder and ½ teaspoon of salt.

Chocolate

Dark, milk, and white chocolate and unsweetened cocoa powder are used in the recipes in this book. There are many brands of chocolate, but try to buy the best you can afford. Semisweet chocolate is a dark chocolate that has at least 35 percent cocoa solids, bittersweet chocolate can have more than 70 percent. The higher the percentage of cocoa solids, the richer the flavor. Milk chocolate contains at least 25 percent cocoa solids and tends to consist of cocoa butter, milk, sugar, and flavorings. White chocolate is made from cocoa butter, milk solids, sugar, flavorings, such as vanilla, and emulsifiers, such as lecithin. For advice on melting chocolate, see page 169.

Butter

The recipes specify either salted or unsalted butter. This enables you to control the amount of salt in the recipe. Do not replace butter with margarine or butter substitutes, because it will affect the texture and flavor.

Sugar & spice

The spices and flavorings used in the recipes in this book include chili powder, ground ginger, ground cardamom seeds, vanilla extract, peppermint extract, and strawberry and raspberry flavorings. Always use what the recipe specifies, because substituting one for another will affect the results.

Sugars add color, flavor, sweetness, and moisture. The recipes in this book use light brown, granulated, superfine (you can make your own by processing the same amount of granulated sugar in a food processor for a minute), and confectioners' sugars and also syrups, such as light corn syrup and glucose syrup. Always use what the recipe specifies, because substituting one for another will affect the results.

Equipment

Mini cupcake liners & muffin cups

Mini cupcake liners and muffin baking cups tend to vary considerably in size. The recipes in this book require paper liners with a bottom diameter of 1¼ inches and 1½ inches. Mini silicone cups are also available in a variety of colors, from subtle to bright. They're dishwasher-proof and reusable, and cakes are easy to remove from them by peeling away the cups. To bake, simply set the silicone cups on a baking sheet instead of in a muffin pan. Neither silicone cups nor paper liners need greasing.

Mini muffin pans

Paper cupcake liners and muffin baking cups must sit comfortably in the pan's sections, which should offer some support but not crease up the paper liners. Mini muffin pans have 12 or 24 sections; if using a 12-section pan, you will need to bake two batches of cakes for some recipes in this book.

Mini sectional cake pans

Both round- and square-section cake pans measure 2 inches in diameter per section and are usually bought in packages of 16, which fit onto a base for baking. Alternatively, bake a large yellow cake and let it stand until firm for 24 hours, then cut out 2-inch circles or squares, using a metal cutter as a guide.

Cookie cutters

Cookie cutters can be used to cut out shapes. Cutters are available in a variety of shapes and sizes and are sometimes sold seasonally, so it's worth collecting your favorite shapes when you see them. If you don't have the right size for the recipe, check your glasses, cups, and saucers and cut around these. You can make pie lids from flower, heart, or circle shapes stamped out with cookie cutters.

Molds for mini desserts

You may have some dishes already, perhaps liqueur glasses, a mini muffin pan, ovenproof ramekins (individual ceramic dishes), or demitasse coffee cups. Additional dishes can be bought from kitchen shops, the chinaware section of a department store, or online. Plastic shot glasses are available from supermarkets and (unlike glass) are suitable for freezing. The dishes used are between ¼ cup and ⅓ cup in volume. Where small silicone muffin cups are used, a measurement has been given for the bottom of the muffin cups; metal mini muffin pans with 12 or 24 cups are also used for some recipes. The liqueur glasses used hold ¼ cup.

Mini Cakes

Baking techniques

Preparing pans

Use wax paper or parchment paper to line pans and melted butter or vegetable oil to grease them.

Lining square pans

Place the pan on parchment paper, draw around the pan, and cut out the paper just inside the lines. Cut a strip the depth of the pan and long enough to fit around the perimeter of the pan, then make a ½-inch fold along one long edge. Grease the pan, using a pastry brush, and fit the strip around the sides so the folded strip sits on the bottom. Snip the folded edge at the corners. Press the paper square into the bottom and grease the paper.

Lining round pan cups

Grease the cups. Cut out circles of parchment paper ½ inch larger than the cup diameters. Make ¼-inch cuts at the sides of the circles and press them in the cups so the snipped edges go up the sides.

Mixing muffins

Muffins are made by adding the wet ingredients to the dry ingredients. The flour is usually sifted first. Add the wet ingredients all at once and fold everything together gently. As soon as they're combined but with specks of flour still visible, spoon the batter into the liners or cups. Overmixing muffins can make them less light.

Filling liners or cups

Unless otherwise stated, fill cupcake liners until they're almost full and the batter is level with the top of the liners. For muffins, the batter can extend above the tops of the cups slightly to achieve the "muffin top."

How to tell if a cake is baked

Cakes are usually slightly domed in the center with a lightly browned surface. Gently touch the surface with your flattened fingers; it should feel just firm. Some cakes require another test: pushing a toothpick into the center; if baked, it will come out clean.

Decorating techniques

Applying frostings & creams

Take a little of the frosting from the bowl, using a small spatula. Spread the frosting gently over each cake to cover it in an even layer before refining the application using the flat edge of a knife to level the surface.

Coloring ready-to-use fondant & marzipan (almond paste)

Using a toothpick, dot a little food coloring onto the fondant. If you want a delicate color, use a tiny amount, because a little goes a long way. Working on a surface dusted with confectioners' sugar, knead in the color.

Covering cakes with ready-to-use fondant

Roll out the required amount of fondant thinly on a surface that is lightly dusted with confectioners' sugar to between ⅛ inch and ¼ inch thick and 3 inches in diameter. Lift over the cake and use your fingers to ease the fondant around the sides, pinching it together where there's a point. Cut off the excess at these points and tuck the fondant around the bottom before trimming off excess with a sharp knife.

Making a paper pastry bag

Cut out a 10-inch square from parchment paper and fold it diagonally in half to make a triangle. Cut the paper in half on one side of the folded line to make two triangles. Holding one triangle with the long edge away from you, curl the right point over to meet the central point, forming a cone. Curl the left point over the cone. Adjust the points so there's no hole at the tip. Fold the points over to secure the cone in place.

Pastry bags & tips

Pastry bags can be fitted with tips or snipped at the tip. Fill the bag halfway with frosting and twist the open end together to seal. Snip off the tip and test the thickness of the piping, snipping off more, if necessary. (If using a piping tip, cut ½ inch off the tip of the bag and fit a tip inside the bag before filling the bag and sealing it.) The tips used in this book are: a large star tip for lavish swirls; a small star tip for small stars or shells; and a writer tip for lines and dots.

Yellow cake

Makes: one 7-inch
round or square cake

Prep: 15 minutes

Cook: 40 minutes

3½ sticks salted butter, softened

¾ cup granulated sugar

1 teaspoon vanilla extract

3 eggs, beaten

1⅓ cups all-purpose flour

1¼ teaspoons baking powder

2 tablespoons milk

When using this moist, buttery yellow cake batter, follow the baking directions in your chosen recipe. To bake it as a yellow cake, put it in a 7-inch round or square, greased and lined cake pan and bake for 40 minutes, or until firm to the touch.

1. Put the butter and sugar in a mixing bowl and beat them together with an electric handheld mixer until pale and fluffy. Beat in the vanilla. Add the eggs, a little at a time, beating between each addition. (If they are added too quickly, the batter will separate and the cake won't be as light.)

2. Sift in the flour and baking powder, then stir it in gently with a metal spoon. As soon as the ingredients are combined, gently stir in the milk. The batter should drop easily from the spoon when tapped on the side of the bowl. (For a shortcut "all-in-one" method, put all the ingredients in the bowl together and beat until soft and creamy.) Bake as per your recipe or turn the batter out into a greased and lined 7-inch cake pan and bake in an oven preheated to 350°F for 40 minutes.

Variations

White chocolate:

Replace half of the sugar with 8 ounces white chocolate, melted, stirring it into the batter after the eggs.

Lemon:

Add the finely grated rind of 2 lemons when creaming the butter and sugar and use 2 tablespoons of lemon juice instead of vanilla and milk.

Orange:

Add the finely grated rind of 1 orange when creaming the butter and sugar and use 2 tablespoons of orange juice instead of vanilla and milk.

Almond:

Replace ½ cup flour with ½ cup ground almonds (almond meal) and add 1 teaspoon of almond extract instead of the vanilla.

Buttercream

Makes: 1 quantity of buttercream

Put 1 stick of unsalted butter in a mixing bowl and beat with an electric handheld mixer until softened. Add 1¼ cups of confectioners' sugar and beat with the mixer until smooth and creamy. Pour in 1 tablespoon of hot water and beat until soft and fluffy. For vanilla buttercream, beat in 1 teaspoon of vanilla extract with the confectioners' sugar. For lemon buttercream, beat in the finely grated rind of 1 lemon with the confectioners' sugar and use 2 tablespoons of lemon juice instead of the water.

Carrot cakes

Makes: 20
Prep: 1 hour, plus cooling
Cook: 35 minutes

Carrot cake is such an all-time favorite that it simply had to be included here. If you're making these in advance, the little marzipan carrots can be positioned after frosting the cake, but don't add the leafy tops more than a few hours before serving, because otherwise they will wilt.

1½ sticks salted butter, softened, plus extra for greasing

¾ cup firmly packed light brown sugar

3 eggs

1¼ cups all-purpose flour

1¾ teaspoons baking powder

½ teaspoon ground allspice

1 cup ground almonds (almond meal)

finely grated rind of 1 lemon

1⅓ cups grated carrots

½ cup coarsely chopped golden raisins

DECORATION

⅔ cup cream cheese

3 tablespoons unsalted butter, softened

1 cup confectioners' sugar, plus extra for dusting

2 tablespoons lemon juice

2 ounces marzipan

orange food coloring

several sprigs of dill

1. Preheat the oven to 350°F. Grease and line the bottom and sides of an 11-inch x 9-inch baking pan. Grease the parchment paper. Put the butter, light brown sugar, eggs, flour, baking powder, allspice, ground almonds, and lemon rind in a mixing bowl and beat with an electric handheld mixer until smooth and creamy. Stir in the carrots and raisins.

2. Turn the batter out into the pan and level the surface. Bake in the preheated oven for 35 minutes, or until risen and just firm to the touch. Let rest in the pan for 10 minutes, then transfer to a wire rack to cool.

3. For the decoration, beat together the cream cheese, butter, confectioners' sugar, and lemon juice until creamy. Color the marzipan deep orange. Roll it into a log shape on a surface lightly dusted with confectioners' sugar, then divide it into 20 pieces and form each one into a small carrot shape, marking shallow grooves around each with a knife.

4. Using a spatula, spread the frosting over the cake almost to the edges. Trim the crusts from the cake to neaten it, then cut it into 20 squares. Place a marzipan carrot on each cake and add a small sprig of dill.

Cherry and almond loaves

Makes: 12
Prep: 15 minutes, plus cooling
Cook: 20 minutes

Here is a bite-size treat for those who like traditional cakes. If you don't have a silicone loaf pan, use individual metal pans — because they are slightly larger, you'll have enough batter for only eight cakes, and these need an extra 5 minutes' cooking time.

6 tablespoons salted butter, softened, plus extra for greasing

⅓ cup granulated sugar

1 egg

1 egg yolk

½ cup all-purpose flour

½ teaspoon baking powder

½ teaspoon almond extract

½ cup ground almonds (almond meal)

¼ cup chopped candied cherries

2 tablespoons slivered almonds

½ cup confectioners' sugar

2 teaspoons lemon juice

1. Preheat the oven to 350°F. Place a 12-section silicone mini loaf pan on a baking sheet, or grease and line the bottom of individual mini loaf pans. Put the butter, granulated sugar, egg, egg yolk, flour, baking powder, almond extract, and ground almonds in a mixing bowl and beat together with an electric handheld mixer until smooth and creamy. Stir in the cherries.

2. Using a teaspoon, spoon the batter into the pan sections and level with the back of the spoon. Break up the slivered almonds slightly by squeezing them in your hands and sprinkle them over the cake batter. Bake in the preheated oven for 20 minutes (25 minutes if using pans), or until risen and just firm to the touch. Let rest in the pan for 5 minutes, then transfer to a wire rack to cool.

3. Beat the confectioners' sugar and lemon juice together in a small bowl and drizzle the icing over the cakes with a teaspoon. Let set.

Mango cakes

Makes: 12

Prep: 15 minutes, plus cooling, plus 2–3 hours soaking

Cook: 20 minutes

½ cup finely chopped dried mango

finely grated rind of 1 orange, plus 3 tablespoons juice

⅓ cup shredded dry unsweetened coconut

6 tablespoons salted butter, softened, plus extra for greasing

⅓ cup granulated sugar

1 egg

⅔ cup all-purpose flour

½ teaspoon baking powder

confectioners' sugar, for dusting

Dried mango and coconut give these little cakes a fresh, tropical flavor, heightened by a hint of orange. They'll keep in an airtight container for several days.

1. Preheat the oven to 350°F. Place a 12-section silicone mini loaf pan on a baking sheet, or grease and line the bottom of individual mini loaf pans. Put the mango and orange juice in a small bowl and let stand, covered, for 2–3 hours, or until the orange juice is mostly absorbed.

2. Put the coconut, butter, sugar, egg, flour, baking powder, and orange rind in a mixing bowl and beat together with an electric handheld mixer until smooth and pale. Stir in the mango and any unabsorbed orange juice.

3. Using a teaspoon, spoon the batter into the pan sections and level with the back of the spoon. Bake in the preheated oven for 20 minutes (25 minutes if using pans), or until risen and just firm to the touch. Let rest in the pan for 5 minutes, then transfer to a wire rack to cool.

4. Serve lightly dusted with confectioners' sugar.

Mini layer cakes

Makes: 12
Prep: 20 minutes, plus cooling
Cook: 15 minutes

5 tablespoons salted butter, softened, plus extra for greasing

⅓ cup granulated sugar

½ cup all-purpose flour

½ teaspoon baking powder

1 egg

1 egg yolk

1 teaspoon vanilla extract

DECORATION

⅔ cup heavy cream

⅓ cup strawberry jelly or preserves

⅔ cup confectioners' sugar

1 tablespoon lemon juice

So tiny and dainty, these "doll's house"-size cakes are just right with a cup of coffee when you don't want anything too rich or filling. Because of their size, they'll dry out quickly, so store them in an airtight container or freeze if making ahead.

1. Preheat the oven to 350°F. Place a 12-cup silicone mini muffin pan on a baking sheet, or grease and line the bottom of a 12-cup mini muffin pan. Put the butter, granulated sugar, flour, baking powder, egg, egg yolk, and vanilla in a mixing bowl and beat together with an electric handheld mixer until it is smooth and creamy.

2. Using a teaspoon, spoon the batter into the pan cups and level with the back of the spoon. Bake in the preheated oven for 15 minutes, or until risen and just firm to the touch. Let stand in the pan for 5 minutes, then transfer to a wire rack to cool.

3. For the decoration, whip the cream until it just holds peaks. Slice the cakes in half horizontally, using a small serrated knife. Set aside 2 tablespoons of the jelly, putting it in a small paper pastry bag and snipping off the tip (see page 10). Sandwich the cakes together with the remaining jelly and the cream.

4. Beat the confectioners' sugar and lemon juice together in a bowl until smooth. Spoon the icing over the cakes, spreading it to the edges. Pipe dots of jelly on each cake and draw a wooden toothpick through them.

Frosted baby Bundt cakes

Makes: 12
Prep: 20 minutes, plus cooling
Cook: 15–20 minutes

This cake recipe is made with cinnamon, walnuts, and apples for a really moist texture. Don't be put off if you don't have mini Bundt pans; any small pans with a similar capacity can be used just as effectively instead.

1⅔ cups all-purpose flour, plus extra for sprinkling

1 teaspoon baking powder

1 teaspoon ground cinnamon, plus extra for sprinkling

⅔ cup granulated sugar

½ cup finely chopped walnuts

2 small Pippin or other cooking apples, peeled, cored, and finely grated

⅓ cup vegetable oil, plus extra for greasing

3 eggs

⅔ cup buttermilk

FROSTING

3 tablespoons plain yogurt

scant 1¼ cups confectioners' sugar, sifted

1. Preheat the oven to 350°F. Brush two mini Bundt pans with six cups with vegetable oil. Sprinkle a little flour into the pans and tilt so that both the bottoms and sides are coated; tap out the excess.

2. Sift the flour, baking powder, and cinnamon into a mixing bowl. Stir in the granulated sugar, walnuts, and apples.

3. In a separate mixing bowl, beat together the oil, eggs, and buttermilk. Add them to the dry ingredients and mix to form a soft paste.

4. Using a teaspoon, spoon the batter into the pans and level with the back of the spoon. Bake in the preheated oven for 15–20 minutes, or until risen and just firm to the touch. Let stand in the pans for 5 minutes, then transfer to a wire rack to cool.

5. For the frosting, put the yogurt into a bowl and add the confectioners' sugar. Beat together until smooth. Spoon a little of the frosting onto the top of each cake, easing it slightly down the sides with the back of the spoon so the frosting runs down the sides. Lightly sprinkle the tops of the cakes with cinnamon.

Coffee crumb cakes

Makes: 18
Prep: 30 minutes, plus cooling
Cook: 30–35 minutes

4 tablespoons salted butter, softened, plus extra for greasing

½ cup granulated sugar

1 egg

⅓ cup sour cream

1 cup all-purpose flour

1 teaspoon baking powder

TOPPING

⅔ cup all-purpose flour

5 tablespoons salted butter, cut into pieces

½ teaspoon ground apple pie spice

1½ teaspoons ground espresso coffee

½ cup granulated sugar

ICING

⅔ cup confectioners' sugar

1 tablespoon strong espresso coffee, cooled

One of these treats is an ideal accompaniment to a mid-morning cup of coffee or tea. The crumb topping is sweet and streusel-like, in delicious contrast to the light and airy cake underneath it.

1. Preheat the oven to 350°F. Grease and line the bottom and sides of a shallow 7-inch square, loose-bottom cake pan. Grease the parchment paper.

2. For the topping, put the all-purpose flour, butter, apple pie spice, and coffee in a food processor and blend until the mixture starts to resemble coarse bread crumbs. Add the granulated sugar and blend again briefly. Turn the mixture into a mixing bowl.

3. For the batter, put the butter, granulated sugar, egg, sour cream, all-purpose flour, and baking powder in the food processor and blend until smooth and creamy, then turn out into the pan and level the surface. Sprinkle the crumb mixture in an even layer on top. Bake in the preheated oven for 30–35 minutes, or until risen and just firm to the touch and a toothpick inserted into the center comes out clean. Let stand in the pan for 10 minutes, then transfer to a wire rack to cool.

4. For the icing, put all but 2 tablespoons of the confectioners' sugar in a small mixing bowl and add the coffee. Beat to a smooth paste that falls in a thick trail from the spoon, adding a little more confectioners' sugar, if necessary. Cut the cake into three even pieces, then cut across to make 18 rectangular pieces. Drizzle with the icing.

gooey chocolate fudge bites

Makes: 21
Prep: 25 minutes, plus cooling
Cook: 35 minutes

2 sticks salted butter, cut into pieces, plus extra for greasing

8 ounces semisweet chocolate, coarsely chopped

½ cup heavy cream

3 eggs

¾ cup firmly packed light brown sugar

¾ cup all-purpose flour

FROSTING

8 ounces semisweet chocolate

3 tablespoons light corn syrup

4 tablespoons unsalted butter, cut into pieces

½ cup confectioners' sugar, sifted

This is as rich and delicious as chocolate cake can get. It's moist and gooey, with a generous amount of chocolate fudge frosting. Store in a cool place, not the refrigerator, so that the texture isn't ruined.

1. Preheat the oven to 325°F. Grease and line the bottom and sides of an 8-inch square cake pan. Grease the parchment paper.

2. Put the butter, chocolate, and cream in a heatproof bowl, set the bowl over a saucepan of gently simmering water, and heat until melted. Let stand to cool slightly.

3. Put the eggs and light brown sugar in a mixing bowl and beat together with an electric handheld mixer until the batter begins to turn frothy. Stir in the cooled chocolate mixture. Sift in the flour and stir it in gently.

4. Turn the batter into the pan and level the surface. Bake in the preheated oven for 35 minutes, or until risen and just firm to the touch. Let stand in the pan for 10 minutes, then transfer to a wire rack to cool.

5. For the frosting, put 6 ounces of the chocolate in a small, heavy saucepan with the syrup and butter. Heat gently, stirring frequently, until the mixture is smooth and glossy. Transfer the mixture to a mixing bowl and beat in the confectioners' sugar. Let stand until the frosting has thickened enough to just hold its shape.

6. Slice the cake in half horizontally and spread half of the fudge frosting on the cut side of the bottom piece. Place the other piece on top, cut side down, and spread the remaining frosting on top of the cake. Using a sharp knife, carefully cut thin shards from the remaining chocolate. (If it's too brittle, heat briefly in the microwave and try again.) Trim off the edges of the cake to neaten it, then cut it into 21 rectangles. Sprinkle the chocolate shards on top.

Chocolate brownies

Makes: 25
Prep: 15 minutes, plus cooling
Cook: 18–20 minutes

1 stick salted butter, cut into
pieces, plus extra for greasing

4 ounces semisweet
chocolate, coarsely chopped

2 eggs

1 cup firmly packed
light brown sugar

2 teaspoons vanilla extract

½ cup all-purpose flour

¼ cup unsweetened cocoa
powder

⅓ cup coarsely chopped pecans
or walnuts

These little brownies have the familiar sugary crust and soft gooey center that we've come to know and love. They're impossible to resist, so it's a good thing they're only bite-size!

1. Preheat the oven to 400°F. Grease and line the bottom and sides of a shallow 7-inch square, loose-bottom cake pan.

2. Put the butter and chocolate in a heatproof bowl, set the bowl over a saucepan of gently simmering water, and heat until melted. Let the mixture stand to cool slightly.

3. Put the eggs, sugar, and vanilla in a mixing bowl and beat together with an electric handheld mixer until the batter begins to turn frothy. Stir in the chocolate mixture until combined.

4 Sift the flour and cocoa into the bowl and sprinkle in the nuts. Stir together gently, then turn the batter into the pan and level the surface.

5. Bake in the preheated oven for 18–20 minutes, or until the crust feels dry but gives a little when gently pressed. (If you're unsure, it's better to slightly undercook brownies because they lose their gooeyness when they are overbaked.) Let stand in the pan for 10 minutes, then transfer to a wire rack to cool. Cut the cake into 25 squares.

Vanilla swirl brownies

Makes: 12
Prep: 20 minutes, plus cooling
Cook: 12–15 minutes

6 tablespoons salted butter,
plus extra for greasing

4 ounces semisweet
chocolate, coarsely chopped

1 egg

1 egg yolk

½ cup firmly packed
light brown sugar

⅓ cup all-purpose flour

½ teaspoon baking powder

3 ounces milk chocolate,
coarsely chopped

FROSTING

⅔ cup mascarpone cheese

¼ cup confectioners' sugar

1 teaspoon vanilla extract

milk or semisweet chocolate
curls, to sprinkle

These rich, chocolatey morsels are great as an afternoon treat — and even better with coffee after a special dinner with friends.

1. Preheat the oven to 375°F. Grease and line the bottom of a 12-cup mini muffin pan.

2. Put the butter and semisweet chocolate in a heatproof bowl, set the bowl over a saucepan of gently simmering water, and heat until melted. Let the mixture stand to cool slightly.

3. Put the egg, egg yolk, and light brown sugar in a mixing bowl and beat together with an electric handheld mixer until the batter begins to turn frothy. Stir in the melted chocolate. Sift the flour and baking powder into the bowl, sprinkle with the milk chocolate, and stir together. Using a teaspoon, spoon the batter into the pan cups.

4. Bake in the preheated oven for 12–15 minutes, or until the crust feels dry but gives a little when gently pressed. (If you're unsure, it's better to slightly undercook brownies because they lose their gooeyness when overbaked.) Let stand in the pan for 10 minutes, then transfer to a wire rack to cool.

5. For the frosting, put the mascarpone cheese, confectioners' sugar, and vanilla in a small bowl and beat with an electric handheld mixer until smooth and creamy. Put the mixture in a pastry bag fitted with a ½-inch tip and pipe swirls over the cakes. Sprinkle with chocolate curls.

Blueberry and vanilla muffins

Makes: 18
Prep: 10 minutes, plus cooling
Cook: 15 minutes

In these fresh blueberry muffins, the plump, juicy fruits burst during baking to color and flavor the light, airy cake. This recipe uses homemade paper liners, made by pressing squares of parchment paper into the muffin pan.

1 cup all-purpose flour

1½ teaspoons baking powder

½ cup granulated sugar

½ cup blueberries

2 teaspoons vanilla extract

1 egg

½ cup buttermilk

2 tablespoons vegetable oil

vanilla sugar, for dusting

1. Preheat the oven to 375°F. Cut out eighteen 3½-inch squares from parchment paper. Push the squares into two 12-cup mini muffin pans, creasing the squares to fit so that they form paper liners. Don't worry if they lift out of the cups slightly; the weight of the muffin batter will hold them in place.

2. Sift the flour and baking powder into a mixing bowl. Stir in the sugar and blueberries. In a separate mixing bowl, beat together the vanilla, egg, buttermilk, and oil with a fork until evenly combined.

3. Turn the buttermilk mixture into the flour. Using a metal spoon, gently fold the ingredients together until only just mixed. (Don't overblend the ingredients or the muffins won't be as light.)

4. Spoon the batter into the paper liners; it should be level with the top of the pan. Sprinkle with a little vanilla sugar and bake in the preheated oven for 15 minutes, or until risen and just firm to the touch. Let the muffins stand in the pan for 2 minutes, then transfer them in their liners to a wire rack to cool. Serve warm or cold, dusted with extra vanilla sugar.

1

2

4

Cranberry muffins

Makes: 18
Prep: 10 minutes, plus cooling
Cook: 12–15 minutes

These muffins can be prepared and baked in less than half an hour, perfect for a relaxed weekend breakfast. For flavor variations, try adding the grated rind of an orange or a sprinkling of ground ginger or cinnamon.

¾ cup all-purpose flour

1 teaspoon baking powder

¼ cup granulated sugar

¾ cup coarsely chopped dried cranberries

½ cup plain yogurt

1 egg

2 tablespoons vegetable oil

confectioners' sugar, for dusting

1. Preheat the oven to 375°F. Line two 12-cup mini muffin pans with eighteen 1¼-inch mini paper liners.

2. Sift the flour and baking powder into a mixing bowl. Stir in the granulated sugar and cranberries. In a separate mixing bowl, beat together the yogurt, egg, and vegetable oil with a fork until evenly combined.

3. Turn the yogurt mixture into the flour. Using a metal spoon, gently fold the ingredients together until only just mixed. (Don't overblend the ingredients or the muffins won't be as light.)

4. Spoon the batter into the paper liners; it should be level with the top of the pan. Bake in the preheated oven for 12–15 minutes, or until risen and just firm to the touch. Let the muffins stand in the pan for 2 minutes, then transfer them in their liners to a wire rack to cool. Serve warm or cold, dusted with confectioners' sugar.

Double chocolate muffins

Makes: 12
Prep: 15 minutes, plus cooling
Cook: 15 minutes

Because these muffins are tiny, it's only right that they're as packed with chocolate as they could be. Any that are not eaten fresh from the oven can be kept for two days in an airtight container. Warm them for a few minutes in a moderate oven to revive their flavor.

2½ tablespoons unsweetened cocoa powder

½ cup all-purpose flour

¾ teaspoon baking powder

2 tablespoons packed light brown sugar

3 ounces coarsely chopped milk chocolate

1 egg

3 tablespoons milk

3 tablespoons salted butter, melted

2 ounces semisweet chocolate, coarsely chopped

1. Preheat the oven to 375°F. Line a 12-cup mini muffin pan with 1¼-inch mini paper liners.

2. Sift the unsweetened cocoa, flour, and baking powder into a mixing bowl. Stir in the light brown sugar and milk chocolate. In a separate mixing bowl, beat together the egg, milk, and butter with a fork until evenly combined.

3. Turn the egg mixture into the flour. Using a metal spoon, gently fold the ingredients together until only just mixed. (Don't overblend the ingredients or the muffins won't be as light.)

4. Spoon the batter into the paper liners; it should be level with the top of the pan. Bake in the preheated oven for 15 minutes, or until risen and just firm to the touch. Let the muffins stand in the pan for 2 minutes, then transfer them in their liners to a wire rack to cool.

5. Put the semisweet chocolate in a heatproof bowl, set over a saucepan of gently simmering water, and heat until melted. Using a teaspoon, drizzle the melted chocolate over the muffins and serve warm or cold.

Maple and banana cupcakes

Makes: 12
Prep: 20 minutes, plus cooling
Cook: 18–20 minutes

1 small banana

2 tablespoons maple syrup

2 tablespoons milk

4½ tablespoons salted butter, softened

½ cup granulated sugar

1 egg, beaten

¾ cup all-purpose flour

¾ teaspoon baking powder

FROSTING

1½ sticks salted butter, softened

1 teaspoon vanilla extract

⅓ cup confectioners' sugar

½ cup maple syrup

8 pecan or walnut halves, coarsely chopped, to decorate

Banana cake invariably appeals to everyone, from tiny tots to adults. These mini ones can be served plain, simply dusted with confectioners' sugar, or swirled with the delicious maple buttercream.

1. Preheat the oven to 350°F. Line a 12-cup mini muffin pan with 1¼-inch mini paper liners.

2. In a small mixing bowl, mash the banana to a puree with a fork. Stir in the maple syrup and milk.

3. Put the butter and granulated sugar in a separate mixing bowl and beat with an electric handheld mixer until light and fluffy. Gradually beat in the egg, a little at a time, adding a teaspoon of the flour if it starts to separate.

4. Sift half of the flour and the baking powder into the bowl with the butter mixture, then add half of the banana. Gently fold the ingredients together until only just mixed. Sift in the remaining flour, add the remaining banana mixture, and fold in.

5. Spoon the batter into the paper liners. Bake in the preheated oven for 18–20 minutes, or until risen and just firm to the touch. Let stand in the pan for 5 minutes, then transfer to a wire rack to cool.

6. For the frosting, put the butter, vanilla, confectioners' sugar, and maple syrup in a bowl and beat with an electric handheld mixer until smooth and creamy. Put the frosting in a small paper pastry bag fitted with a ½-inch star tip and use to decorate the cupcakes. Sprinkle with nuts.

Baby shower cupcakes

Makes: 18
Prep: 45 minutes, plus cooling
Cook: 15 minutes

5 tablespoons salted butter, softened

½ cup granulated sugar

1 egg

1 egg yolk

½ cup all-purpose flour

½ teaspoon baking powder

1 teaspoon vanilla extract

DECORATION

1 quantity Buttercream (see page 11)

pink and blue food colorings

2 ounces ready-to-use fondant

confectioners' sugar, for dusting

These are so simple to make, but very pretty — and perfect for the next baby shower. Pink and blue look effective together, but you can change the colors to any other combination.

1. Preheat the oven to 350°F. Line two 12-cup mini muffin pans with eighteen 1¼-inch mini paper liners, preferably in deep pink or blue.

2. Put the butter, granulated sugar, egg, egg yolk, flour, baking powder, and vanilla in a mixing bowl and beat together with an electric handheld mixer until smooth and creamy. Spoon the mixture into the paper liners. Bake in the preheated oven for 15 minutes, or until risen and just firm to the touch. Let stand in the pans for 5 minutes, then transfer to a wire rack to cool.

3. For the decoration, divide the buttercream equally between two bowls and color one with pink coloring and the other with blue, so they're pale pastel. Using a spatula, spread a thin layer of pink frosting over half of the cakes and blue over the other half, reserving some for decoration.

4. Color the remaining buttercream in the bowls to a deeper tone and put it in small paper pastry bags fitted with ½-inch star tips. Pipe pink shells around the blue cakes and blue shells around the pink ones.

5. Color half the ready-to-use fondant blue (see page 10) and wrap it tightly in plastic wrap. Color the remainder pink and roll it out thinly on a surface lightly dusted with confectioners' sugar.

6. Cut the pink fondant into ½-inch-wide strips, then cut across these at 1-inch intervals to make tiny rectangles. Use two rectangles to shape bow ends, pinching the ends together as you position them on the blue-edge cakes. Bend two more rectangles into loops, pinching the ends together, and secure with a damp paintbrush to complete each bow. Use the blue fondant in the same way to make bows for the pink-edge cakes.

Chocolate and raspberry cupcakes

Makes: 20

Prep: 50 minutes, plus cooling

Cook: 12–15 minutes

½ cup raspberries

½ cup unsweetened
cocoa powder

½ cup boiling water

4 tablespoons salted butter,
softened

⅔ cup firmly packed
light brown sugar

1 egg, beaten

¾ cup all-purpose flour

¾ teaspoon baking powder

DECORATION

3 tablespoons salted butter

4 ounces semisweet chocolate,
coarsely chopped

2 tablespoons light corn syrup

⅓ cup raspberries

½ cup confectioners' sugar

Here's your chance to get carried away with special messages on these pretty cakes — hearts, kisses, whatever you desire! Once decorated, they'll keep fresh for a couple of days in a cool place.

1. Preheat the oven to 350°F. Line two 12-cup mini muffin pans with twenty 1¼-inch mini paper liners, preferably in deep pink or brown.

2. Put the raspberries in a small mixing bowl and crush with a fork until they are broken up. In a separate mixing bowl, whisk the unsweetened cocoa with the boiling water. Let stand to cool.

3. Put the butter and light brown sugar in a third mixing bowl and beat together with an electric handheld mixer until light and fluffy. Beat in the egg a little at a time.

4. Stir in the flour, baking powder, and the cocoa mixture until evenly combined, then add the raspberries and mix together lightly. Spoon the batter into the paper liners. Bake in the preheated oven for 12–15 minutes, or until risen and just firm to the touch. Let stand in the pans for 5 minutes, then transfer to a wire rack to cool.

5. For the decoration, melt the butter in a small saucepan and add the chocolate and syrup. Heat gently until the chocolate has almost melted, then turn into a mixing bowl. Let stand to cool, stirring frequently, until the mixture has thickened enough to almost hold its shape. Spoon it over the cakes and spread to the edges, using a spatula.

6. Crush the raspberries and press them through a strainer, using the back of a spoon to extract the juice. Sift the confectioners' sugar over the juice and stir to make a loose paste. Put the icing in a small paper pastry bag and snip off the tip (see page 10). Pipe hearts and kisses onto the cakes.

Red velvet heart cupcakes

Makes: 12

Prep: 1–1½ hours, plus cooling

Cook: 15 minutes

1 small raw beet, finely grated

1 egg

2 tablespoons buttermilk
or sour cream

1 teaspoon vinegar

4 tablespoons salted butter,
softened

¼ cup firmly packed
light brown sugar

⅔ cup all-purpose flour

2 teaspoons unsweetened
cocoa powder

½ teaspoon baking powder

DECORATION

½ quantity Buttercream
(see page 11)

2½ ounces ready-to-use fondant

deep red food coloring

confectioners' sugar, for dusting

These cakes take a little while to decorate, but the results will certainly be worth the effort. Make yourself comfortable and enjoy!

1. Preheat the oven to 350°F. Line a 12-cup mini muffin pan with 1¼-inch mini paper liners in deep red or white.

2. Put the beet, egg, buttermilk, and vinegar in a mixing bowl and stir together until well combined. Put the butter and brown sugar in a separate mixing bowl and beat together with an electric handheld mixer until pale and fluffy. Sift half of the flour and unsweetened cocoa and the baking powder into the butter mixture and turn in the beet mixture. Stir gently until evenly combined. Sift in the remaining flour and cocoa and stir to mix.

3. Spoon the batter into the paper liners. Bake in the preheated oven for 15 minutes, or until risen and just firm to the touch. Let stand in the pan for 5 minutes, then transfer to a wire rack to cool.

4. For the decoration, spread the buttercream over the cakes, using a spatula. Color the ready-to-use fondant a deep red (see page 10).

5. Divide the fondant into 12 even pieces. Roll a piece of fondant into a thin rope 4½ inches long. On a surface lightly dusted with confectioners' sugar, flatten it with a rolling pin, keeping it no more than ½-inch wide. Cut it in half lengthwise, then across into 1-inch pieces. Repeat with the remaining fondant. Roll each little piece up between your thumb and finger to resemble a tiny rose. Use the roses to build heart shapes on top of all the cakes by pressing them gently down into the buttercream.

Summer flower cupcakes

Makes: 16
Prep: 2½ hours, plus cooling
Cook: 25 minutes

These little cakes are a labor of love, but they look simply stunning. If you've planned a color theme for a special party, you can alter the colors of the vertical stripes to enhance it. Once decorated, they'll keep in a cool place for several days.

a little salted butter,
for greasing

1 quantity Lemon Cake batter
(see page 11)

1 quantity Lemon Buttercream
(see page 11)

2 pounds white ready-to-use
fondant

pink and purple food colorings

confectioners' sugar, for dusting

1. Preheat the oven to 350°F. Grease and line the bottom of a cake pan containing sixteen 2-inch cups.

2. Put 2 teaspoons of the cake batter into each pan cup. Bake in the preheated oven for 25 minutes, or until risen and just firm to the touch. Let stand in the pan for 5 minutes before carefully loosening each cake by running a slender knife around the sides of each cup. Transfer the cakes to a wire rack to cool before peeling away the lining paper.

3. Reserve 3 tablespoons of the buttercream and use the remainder to spread a thin layer over the tops and sides of the cakes.

4. Reserve one-third of the ready-to-use fondant. From the remainder, color one-third pale pink, one-third purple, and one-third a darker pink (see page 10). Take half of each colored fondant and roll it out thinly on a surface lightly dusted with confectioners' sugar. Cut a strip from each color that is the depth of the cakes. Cut this into ¼-inch-wide strips the depth of the cake and secure them, in alternating colors, around the sides of the cakes, pressing them gently into the buttercream. Use the remaining colored fondant to cover all the cakes.

5. Roll out the reserved white ready-to-use fondant as thinly as possible on a surface lightly dusted with confectioners' sugar and cut out simple flower shapes, using a ½-inch plunger cutter. Press each cut flower shape out onto your finger and then place it on a cake. Repeat until you've built up a cluster of flowers on one cake, then repeat for all the cakes.

6. Color the reserved buttercream pink. Put it in a small paper pastry bag and snip off the tip (see page 10). Pipe little dots in the centers of all the white flowers.

White party stars

Makes: 9–10
Prep: 1–1 ½ hours, plus cooling
Cook: 25–30 minutes

unsalted butter, for greasing

1 quantity Lemon Cake
batter (see page 11)

1 quantity Lemon Buttercream
(see page 11)

1 pound white ready-to-use
fondant

1 egg white

1⅔ cups confectioners' sugar,
sifted, plus extra for dusting

lilac food coloring

These pretty little stars would make a great addition to a special occasion; you could substitute the color of your choice to tie in with your party theme.

1. Preheat the oven to 350°F. Grease and line the bottom and sides of an 11-inch x 9-inch baking pan.

2. Turn the cake batter into the pan and level the surface. Bake in the preheated oven for 25–30 minutes, or until risen and just firm to the touch. Let stand in the pan for 10 minutes, then transfer to a wire rack to cool.

3. If the cake has risen in the center, cut off a thin slice with a large knife. Using a 3-inch star cutter as a guide, cut out shapes from the cake. (Cut each star shape as close to the previously cut star as possible so you don't waste any cake; freeze the cake trimmings for making Mini Cake Pops, see page 58, another time.) Turn the cakes over so that the bottom forms a flat top.

4. Using a spatula, spread a thin layer of buttercream over the top and sides of each star.

5. Divide the ready-to-use fondant into nine or ten equal pieces (depending on the number of stars you cut from the cake). Roll out a piece of the fondant on a surface lightly dusted with confectioners' sugar to a circle about 4½ inches in diameter. Lift it over a star cake and fit the sides, pinching the fondant together at the points. Cut off the excess at the points and then cut around the bottom of the cake. Repeat with the remaining cakes.

6. Beat the egg white in a clean bowl with the half of the confectioners' sugar until smooth. Gradually work in the remaining confectioners' sugar until softly forming peaks. Add a little lilac food coloring and put the icing in a small paper pastry bag fitted with a little writer tip (see page 10). Pipe tiny dots in the center of the tops of the cakes.

Birthday balloons

Makes: 24
Prep: 1–1½ hours, plus cooling
Cook: 18–20 minutes

1 quantity White Chocolate Cake
batter (see page 11)

2 quantities Buttercream
(see page 11)

12 ounces small chewy taffy-style
candies in three different
flavors, such as strawberry,
orange, and lemon

24 (2½-inch) lollipop sticks

4 ounces small red, green,
and yellow sugar-coated
chocolate candies

Kids will love these fun, colorful cakes, lavishly decorated with tempting treats. Use candles to replace some of the balloons if you prefer.

1. Preheat the oven to 350°F. Line two 12-cup mini muffin pans with 1½-inch mini paper liners, preferably in pink, green, or yellow.

2. Spoon the cake batter into the paper liners. Bake in the preheated oven for 18–20 minutes, until risen and just firm to the touch. Let stand in the pan for 5 minutes, then transfer to a wire rack to cool.

3. Using a spatula, spread a thin layer of buttercream over the cakes.

4. For each balloon, take about two of the chewy candies of the same color and mold them into a ball. (If they are brittle or too firm to shape, first microwave them on medium power for 5–6 seconds to soften them. Don't overheat them or they'll turn to a molten syrup.) Push each balloon shape onto the end of a lollipop stick. Pinch the candy around the stick to create the effect of a knotted end. Repeat until you have enough balloons, pushing each into a cake.

5. For the streamers, soften the remaining chewy candies as above and roll them out thinly. Cut them into 2-inch x ¼-inch pieces and curl each one around a lollipop stick. Twist the candies off the sticks and arrange them on the cakes. Sprinkle with the sugar-coated candies to finish.

4

5

Mini party cakes

Makes: 16
Prep: 1¼ hours, plus cooling
Cook: 40 minutes

A platter of these delicious cakes looks impressive at any special get-together. Make them a couple of days in advance, so you've got time to enjoy the decorating before more pressing party tasks arise. For a big birthday, use number sparklers, too.

a little salted butter,
for greasing

1 quantity Yellow Cake batter
(see page 11)

1 quantity Vanilla Buttercream
(see page 11)

heart-shape sugar sprinkles

pearl balls

1. Preheat the oven to 350°F. Grease and line the bottom and sides of a 7-inch square cake pan.

2. Spoon the cake batter into the pan and level the surface with the back of the spoon. Bake in the preheated oven for 40 minutes, or until risen and just firm to the touch. Let stand in the pan for 10 minutes, then transfer to a wire rack to cool.

3. Cut a ¼-inch crust off the edges of the cake, then cut the cake into 16 even squares.

4. Put the buttercream in a paper pastry bag fitted with a small star tip (see page 10). Place the cakes in paper cake liners.

5. Pipe vertical lines down the sides and over the top edges of the cakes. Sprinkle the tops of the cakes with sugar sprinkles and pearl balls.

Halloween cakes

Makes: 18
Prep: 1½ hours, plus cooling
Cook: 40 minutes

a little salted butter,
for greasing

2 quantities Orange Cake batter
(see page 11)

2 tablespoons lemon juice

2 tablespoons orange juice

3 tablespoons honey

⅓ cup apricot preserves or jam

2 tablespoons hot water

orange food coloring

1½ pounds white ready-to-use
fondant

confectioners' sugar, for dusting

2 ounces semisweet chocolate,
coarsely chopped

several soft green jelly candies

20 small Oreo cookies, filling
removed

Serve these cakes at a Halloween party, or box them up for impressive "take home" gifts. They look particularly stunning on a dark plate or cloth.

1. Preheat the oven to 350°F. Grease and line the bottom and sides of a 10½-inch x 8½-inch baking pan. Grease the parchment paper.

2. Turn the cake batter into the pan and level the surface. Bake in the preheated oven for 40 minutes, or until risen and just firm to the touch. Let stand in the pan for 10 minutes, then transfer to a wire rack to cool.

3. If the cake has risen in the center, cut off a thin slice with a large knife. Using a 2½-inch crescent cutter, cut out shapes from the cake. Turn the cakes over so that the bottom forms a flat top.

4. Mix the juices with the honey in a small bowl and drizzle over the surface of the cakes so the syrup seeps into them. Press the preserves through a small strainer into a bowl and stir in the hot water. Brush this mixture over the tops and sides of the cakes.

5. Knead orange food coloring into the ready-to-use fondant (see page 10). Divide the fondant into 18 equal pieces. Roll out a piece of fondant on a surface lightly dusted with confectioners' sugar to a 6-inch x 4-inch oval. Lift it over a crescent cake and fit it around the sides, pinching the fondant together at the points. Cut off the excess at these points and then cut around the bottom of the cake. Repeat with the remaining cakes, reserving the fondant trimmings.

6. Put the chocolate in a heatproof bowl, set the bowl over a saucepan of gently simmering water, and heat until melted. Put the chocolate in a small paper pastry bag and snip off the tip (see page 10). Color the fondant trimmings a deeper orange and shape them into small balls. Mark "pumpkin" ridges with the back of a knife. Cut small pieces of soft jelly candies and push them into the tops for stems, securing with chocolate.

7. To shape bats, heat an Oreo cookie in the microwave until it's soft (this will take 1½–2 minutes, but check after a minute). Cut a circle from one side with a 1-inch cutter. Cut small flutes from the opposite sides with a ½-inch cutter. Secure the decorations in place with chocolate and pipe bat eyes and extra bats around the sides of the cakes.

Party presents

Makes: 16
Prep: 1½ hours, plus cooling
and decorating
Cook: 45 minutes

a little salted butter,
for greasing

1 quantity White Chocolate
or Almond Cake batter
(see page 11)

1 quantity Buttercream
(see page 11)

½ cup apricot preserves or jam

2 tablespoons brandy, almond or
orange liqueur, or water

2 pounds white marzipan

yellow, blue, and pink food
colorings

confectioners' sugar, for dusting

2 ounces white chocolate,
coarsely chopped

3 yards deep pink ribbon,
about ½-inch wide

3 yards yellow ribbon,
about ¼-inch wide

Marzipan makes a wonderful cake covering, particularly for those who find the sweetness of fondant too much. It can be colored, rolled, cut out, and shaped just as you would with ready-to-use fondant, and it is equally fun to work with.

1. Preheat the oven to 350°F. Grease and line the bottom and sides of a 7-inch square cake pan. Turn the cake batter out into the pan and level the surface. Bake in the preheated oven for 45 minutes, or until risen and just firm to the touch. Let stand in the pan for 10 minutes, then transfer to a wire rack to cool.

2. If the cake has risen in the center, cut off a thin slice with a large knife so that the surface of the cake is level. Slice the cake in half horizontally and sandwich the halves together with the buttercream. Cut a ¼-inch crust off the sides. Turn the cake over and check that it's completely level. Cut the cake into 16 even squares.

3. Press the preserves through a small strainer into a little saucepan and stir in the brandy. Heat gently until smooth. Color 1 ounce of the marzipan yellow (see page 10) and another 1 ounce blue and reserve both, wrapped separately in plastic wrap. Color the remaining marzipan pink. Brush the apricot glaze all over the tops and sides of the cake squares.

4. Divide the pink marzipan into 16 even pieces. Roll out a piece of the pink marzipan thinly on a surface lightly dusted with confectioners' sugar, to a 4½-inch square. Lift it over a cake and fit it down the sides, pinching the excess together at the corners. Cut off the excess at these corners and then cut around the bottom of the cake. Repeat with the remaining cakes, reserving the marzipan trimmings.

5. Color the marzipan trimmings a deeper shade of pink and use, with the other colored marzipans, to shape simple gifts. Arrange on the cakes.

6. Put the chocolate in a heatproof bowl, set the bowl over a saucepan of gently simmering water, and heat until melted. Put the melted chocolate in a small paper pastry bag and snip off the tip (see page 10). Pipe lines over the gifts and around the top edges of the cakes. Cut the pink ribbon into 7½-inch lengths and secure around the bottom of the cakes with dots of chocolate from the pastry bag. Cut the yellow ribbon into the same lengths and place these so they sit in the center of the pink ribbon, again secured with dots of the chocolate.

Mini ivory wedding cakes

Makes: 16
Prep: 1½ hours, plus cooling
Cook: 1 hour

Make these pretty cakes for a girls' night before the big day, or, of course, for the wedding party itself. Bake the cakes a day before decorating so they have time to become firm. Assemble the cakes a day before the party.

a little salted butter,
for greasing

2 quantities White Chocolate
Cake batter (see page 11)

9 ounces white ready-to-use
fondant

brown or ivory food coloring

confectioners' sugar, for dusting

16 round, silver cake boards,
about 3 inches in diameter

1¼ cups heavy cream

11 ounces white chocolate,
coarsely chopped

10 yards wired organza ribbon,
about 1 inch wide

1. Preheat the oven to 350°F. Grease and line the bottom and sides of a 9-inch square cake pan.

2. Spoon two-thirds of the cake batter into the pan and level the surface with the back of the spoon. Bake in the preheated oven for 35 minutes, or until well risen and just firm to the touch. Let stand in the pan for 10 minutes, then transfer to a wire rack to cool. Wash and reline the pan and bake the remaining batter for 20–25 minutes, as before.

3. Color the ready-to-use fondant with a dash of brown food coloring (see page 10). Roll out half of the fondant as thinly as possible on a surface lightly dusted with confectioners' sugar. Cut out eight circles, using a 3-inch cookie cutter, rerolling the trimmings to make enough. Repeat with the other half. Dampen the surfaces of the cake boards and position a circle of fondant on each.

4. To make a ganache, heat half of the cream in a small saucepan until hot but not boiling. Pour it into a mixing bowl and add the chocolate. Let stand, stirring frequently, until the chocolate has melted. Let cool completely. Stir in the remaining cream and beat lightly with an electric handheld mixer on slow speed until the ganache is just thick enough to hold its shape. (If overmixed, the mixture might separate.)

5. Using a 2-inch round cookie cutter as a guide, cut out 16 circles from the deeper cake. Use a 1½-inch round cutter as a guide to cut out 16 circles from the shallower cake. (Freeze the trimmings for making trifle or Mini Cake Pops, see page 58, another time.) Place the larger cakes on the boards with the fondant, securing with a little ganache. Spread some of the remaining ganache over the tops and sides of these cakes with a spatula. Position the smaller cakes on top and cover these with ganache in the same way. Let set in a cool place for 1–2 hours.

6. Cut the ribbon into 2-foot lengths and wrap a length around each cake, securing at the tops with bows and cutting off any long ends.

Mini cake pops

Makes: 24
Prep: 1–1¼ hours, plus setting
Cook: 40 minutes

1 quantity Yellow or Almond
Cake, baked (see page 11),
or 1 pound store-bought
yellow cake

⅓ cup mascarpone cheese

½ cup confectioners' sugar

½ teaspoon vanilla or
almond extract

DECORATION

8 ounces milk chocolate,
coarsely chopped

24 lollipop sticks

1¼ cups confectioners' sugar

pink food coloring

4 teaspoons cold water

24 small candies, such as
miniature sugar-coated
chocolate candies

sugar sprinkles

These mini "cupcake" cake pops have both child and adult appeal, so they're ideal for a gathering of mixed ages. Once iced, they'll keep in a cool place for a couple of days.

1. Line a baking sheet with parchment paper. Crumble the yellow cake into a mixing bowl. Add the mascarpone, confectioners' sugar, and vanilla and mix together until you have a thick paste.

2. Divide the paste into 24 even pieces. Roll one piece of the paste into a ball. Push this ball into a mini paper liner, pressing it down so that when it is removed from the liner you have a mini cupcake shape. Shape the remaining 23 cake pops in the same way. Place on the baking sheet and chill for 1–2 hours until firm.

3. Put the chocolate in a heatproof bowl, set the bowl over a saucepan of gently simmering water, and heat until melted. Remove from the heat. Push a lollipop stick into each cake pop. Dip a cake pop into the chocolate, turning it until coated. Lift it from the bowl, letting the excess drip back into the bowl, then place it in a cup or glass. Repeat with the remaining cake pops. Chill or let stand in a cool place until the chocolate has set.

4. Put the confectioners' sugar in a mixing bowl and beat in a dash of pink food coloring and the water until smooth. The icing should almost hold its shape. Spoon a little onto a cake pop, easing it slightly down the sides with the side of a teaspoon. If the icing is too firm, you might need to add a dash more water. Before the icing sets, place a small candy in the center of each cake pop and sprinkle with sugar sprinkles.

3

4

Chocolate mint cake pops

Makes: 26–28
Prep: 1 hour, plus setting
Cook: 5 minutes

11 ounces semisweet
chocolate, coarsely chopped

2 tablespoons unsalted butter,
softened

2 ounces hard mint candies

1 pound milk chocolate

1 cup coarsely chopped mini
marshmallows

26–28 (2½-inch) lollipop sticks

chocolate sprinkles,
to decorate

This cake pop version of "rocky road" is as easy to make as it gets! The milk chocolate coating has family appeal, but you can use semisweet chocolate instead for a more adult flavor.

1. Line a baking sheet with parchment paper. Put the semisweet chocolate in a heatproof bowl, set the bowl over a saucepan of gently simmering water, and heat until melted. Stir in the butter. Let stand until the mixture is cool but not beginning to set.

2. Put the mint candies in a plastic bag and tap firmly with a rolling pin until they are broken into tiny pieces. Finely chop 6 ounces of the milk chocolate, then stir it into the melted semisweet chocolate with the mints and marshmallows until thoroughly mixed.

3. As soon as the mixture is firm enough to hold its shape, divide and roll into 26–28 even balls. Place the balls on the baking sheet and chill in the refrigerator for 30–60 minutes, until firm but not brittle. Push a lollipop stick into each cake pop, then chill for an additional 10 minutes.

4. Coarsely chop the remaining milk chocolate and melt as above, then remove from the heat. Dip a cake pop into the chocolate, turning it until coated. Lift it from the bowl, letting the excess drip back into the bowl, and place it in a cup or glass. Sprinkle with the chocolate sprinkles. Repeat with the remaining cake pops. Chill or let stand in a cool place until the chocolate has set.

Double chocolate whoopie pies

Makes: 12–14

Prep: 25 minutes, plus cooling

Cook: 10 minutes

5 tablespoons salted butter, softened

⅔ cup firmly packed light brown sugar

1 egg

1 teaspoon vanilla extract

1 cup all-purpose flour

½ teaspoon baking soda

⅓ cup unsweetened cocoa powder

⅓ cup buttermilk

FILLING

8 ounces milk chocolate, coarsely chopped

½ cup unsalted butter, softened

⅔ cup confectioners' sugar

3 ounces semisweet chocolate, coarsely chopped

chocolate sprinkles, optional

Quench your chocolate craving with these moist, homemade whoopies; they're so good they'll be gone before you know it!

1. Preheat the oven to 400°F. Line two baking sheets with parchment paper. Put the salted butter, light brown sugar, egg, and vanilla in a mixing bowl and beat together with an electric handheld mixer until the mixture is thickened and pale.

2. Sift the flour, baking soda, and cocoa into a separate mixing bowl. Add half of this mixture and half of the buttermilk to the butter mixture. Stir with a spatula or large metal spoon. Once combined, add the remaining flour mixture and buttermilk and carefully stir again.

3. Put the batter into a large pastry bag fitted with a ½-inch plain tip (see page 10). Pipe small mounds onto the baking sheets, slicing off the peaks with a small knife and spacing the mounds about 2 inches apart to allow for expansion.

4. Bake in the preheated oven for 10 minutes, or until risen and just firm to the touch, switching over the baking sheets halfway through baking. Let stand on the sheets for 5 minutes, then transfer to a wire rack to cool.

5. For the filling, put the milk chocolate in a heatproof bowl, set the bowl over a saucepan of gently simmering water, and heat until melted. Let stand to cool slightly. Put the unsalted butter and confectioners' sugar in a mixing bowl and beat with an electric handheld mixer until light and fluffy. Stir the melted chocolate into the butter mixture until evenly combined.

6. Using the filling, sandwich the whoopie pies together in pairs. Melt the semisweet chocolate as above, then drizzle a little of it over each whoopie pie. Sprinkle with the sprinkles, if using. Let stand in a cool place for a couple of hours until firm.

Gingerbread and vanilla whoopie pies

Makes: 14
Prep: 25 minutes, plus cooling
Cook: 10 minutes

1 egg

⅓ cup firmly packed
light brown sugar

1 tablespoon molasses

3 tablespoons salted butter,
melted

5 tablespoons milk

1¼ cups all-purpose flour

½ teaspoon baking soda

1½ teaspoons ground ginger

½ teaspoon ground allspice

FILLING

½ cup cream cheese

1 tablespoon unsalted butter,
softened

1 teaspoon vanilla extract

½ cup confectioners' sugar,
plus extra for dusting

1 teaspoon boiling water

These whoopies have a distinctive gingerbread flavor, perfect for wintertime comfort eating!

1. Preheat the oven to 350°F. Line two baking sheets with parchment paper. Put the egg, light brown sugar, and molasses in a mixing bowl and beat together with an electric handheld mixer until thickened and foamy. Beat in the salted butter and milk.

2. Sift the flour, baking soda, ginger, and allspice into the bowl and stir with a wooden spoon to make a soft paste.

3. Spoon teaspoons of the batter onto the baking sheets, flattening them slightly so each spoonful is about 1¼ inches in diameter. Space the spoonfuls about 2 inches apart to allow for expansion.

4. Bake in the preheated oven for 10 minutes, or until risen and firm to the touch, switching over the baking sheets halfway through baking. Let stand on the sheets for 5 minutes, then transfer to a wire rack to cool.

5. For the filling, put the cream cheese, unsalted butter, vanilla, and confectioners' sugar in a mixing bowl and beat together with an electric handheld mixer until smooth and creamy. Beat in the boiling water to soften. Using the filling, sandwich the whoopie pies together in pairs. Let stand in a cool place for a couple of hours until firm, then dust with confectioners' sugar.

Mini Pies

Flaky pie dough

Makes: 1 pound 6 ounces, enough
for 12 muffin-size pies
or 1 quantity pie dough

Prep: 25 minutes

2¾ cups plus 2 tablespoons
all-purpose flour, plus extra
for dusting

¼ cup superfine sugar,
optional

6 tablespoons unsalted butter,
chilled and diced

⅓ cup vegetable shortening,
chilled and diced

4–4½ tablespoons cold water

The most versatile, everyday pie dough, this is great for sweet pies. Mix by hand or process in a food processor. The key is to use just enough water to bind the pastry for a wonderful crumbly texture that melts in the mouth.

1. To make by hand, put the flour and sugar in a mixing bowl, then add the butter and shortening. Toss together, then lift the mixture and rub it through your fingers and thumbs. Continue scooping up the mixture and rubbing until it looks like bread crumbs. Gradually mix in the water with a blunt knife, then squeeze the mixture together with your hands until it forms a smooth dough.

To make with an electric mixer or food processor, put the flour, sugar, butter, and shortening in a bowl and mix together, using the electric mixer, or add to a processor bowl fitted with a plastic or metal blade and mix briefly. It should resemble bread crumbs. Gradually add the water with the machine running and mix briefly until it just comes together in a ball.

2. Wrap the pie dough in plastic wrap or put it into a small plastic bag, and chill in the refrigerator for 15 mins, then roll out and use as instructed in the recipe.

Tips

Keep everything as cold as possible. Use butter and vegetable shortening straight from the refrigerator. If your hands feel hot, rinse them in cold water before you begin. Use cold water to bind. A marble pastry board is useful (but not essential) for keeping the pastry cold while rolling out.

Don't add too much liquid. Use just enough to bind the crumbs. For making smaller quantities of pie dough, add water using teaspoons, although for larger quantities, you can change to tablespoons. Err on the side of caution; if you use too much water, the pastry will be hard.

Avoid overdusting the work surface with flour. Aim for the lightest of dustings and rub a little flour over the rolling pin. Before turning the pastry, loosen it with a long, flexible spatula.

All-butter pie dough

Makes: 1 pound 7 ounces, enough for 12 muffin-size pies, or 1 quantity pie dough
Prep: 25 minutes

2¾ cups plus 2 tablespoons all-purpose flour, plus extra for dusting

⅔ cup confectioners' sugar

1½ sticks unsalted butter, at room temperature, diced

4 egg yolks

Based on French "pâte sucrée," this pie dough has more sugar than flaky pie dough, is made with all butter, and is bound with egg yolks for richness.

1. To make by hand, spoon the flour onto the work surface, then sprinkle the sugar over the top. Mix together, then make a well in the center and add the butter and yolks. Work the butter and yolks together with the fingers of one hand. Gradually, draw in a little flour, working your fingertips in a circular motion but being careful not to let the yolk escape through the flour; use your other hand to flick a little flour around the edges so the yolks stay contained. Blend until almost all of the flour has been incorporated, then knead in the last remaining flour until you have a smooth ball.

To make with an electric mixer or food processor, put the sugar and butter in a bowl and mix together, using the electric mixer, or add to a processor bowl fitted with a plastic or metal blade and mix briefly. Add the egg yolks and a little of the flour and beat until smooth, then add the remaining flour and mix to make a smooth dough.

2. Wrap in plastic wrap or put into a small plastic bag, chill in the refrigerator for 15 minutes, then roll out and shape as instructed in the recipe.

Tips
This pie dough requires careful handling. Always chill it when it is first made, and again when it is shaped. If it is too soft to roll out, roll it out thinly between two sheets of parchment paper.

Variations for Flaky pastry & All-butter pastry

Cinnamon:	Add 1 teaspoon of ground cinnamon with the sugar.
Chocolate:	Make with 2⅔ cups all-purpose flour and ¼ cup sifted unsweetened cocoa powder.
Hazelnut:	Toast ⅓ cup hazelnuts until golden. Chop them finely and add with the sugar.
Lemon/Orange:	Add grated rind of 1 lemon or orange with the sugar.

Summer fruit pies

Makes: 24 mini muffin-size pies
Prep: 30 minutes
Cook: 15 minutes

a little butter, for greasing

12 ounces mixed berries, such as
strawberries and raspberries

2 teaspoons cornstarch

3 tablespoons superfine or
granulated sugar, plus extra
for sprinkling

grated rind of ½ lemon

⅔ quantity flaky pie dough
(see page 68) or 1 pound store-
bought rolled dough pie crust,
chilled

a little all-purpose flour,
for dusting

1 egg yolk mixed with
1 tablespoon water, to glaze

whipped cream, to serve

Celebrate the summer with these gorgeous red fruit pies. The soft berries contrast deliciously with the crisp pastry.

1. Preheat the oven to 350°F. Lightly grease two 12-cup mini muffin pans.

2. Hull and coarsely chop the strawberries and break up any large raspberries. Put all the fruit in a mixing bowl and stir in the cornstarch, sugar, and lemon rind.

3. Roll out the pie dough thinly on a lightly floured surface. Using a fluted cookie cutter, stamp out 24 circles, each 2½ inches in diameter. Press them gently into the prepared pans, rerolling the trimmings as needed. Reserve some of the trimmings for decoration.

4. Brush the top edges of the pastry shells with a little of the egg glaze, then spoon in the filling.

5. Roll the reserved pie dough out thinly on a lightly floured surface. Cut strips ½ inch wide. Arrange two strips over each pie, pressing the edges together well to seal, then use a cookie cutter to cut small stars and arrange these over the strips. Brush egg glaze over the pastry and sprinkle with a little sugar.

6. Bake in the preheated oven for 15 minutes, or until golden. Let stand to cool in the pans for 10 minutes, then loosen with a blunt knife and transfer to a wire rack to cool. Serve warm or cold with whipped cream.

Valentine berry love pies

Makes: 24 mini muffin-size pies
Prep: 30 minutes
Cook: 15 minutes

a little butter, for greasing

12 ounces strawberries

2 teaspoon cornstarch

2 tablespoons strawberry jelly
or preserves

grated rind of 2 limes

⅔ quantity all-butter pie
dough (see page 69) or
1 pound store-bought rolled
dough pie crust, chilled

a little all-purpose flour,
for dusting

1 egg yolk mixed with
1 tablespoon water, to glaze

a little superfine or granulated
sugar, for sprinkling

TO SERVE

1 cup heavy cream

grated rind of 2 limes

2 tablespoons confectioners'
sugar

These dainty pies are delicious while warm. If you can find a passion fruit in the grocery store, cut it in half and scoop out the seeds over the whipped cream topping just before serving.

1. Preheat the oven to 350°F. Lightly grease two 12-cup mini muffin pans.

2. Hull and coarsely chop the strawberries. Put them in a mixing bowl and stir in the cornstarch, jelly, and lime rind.

3. Roll half of the pie dough out thinly on a lightly floured surface. Using a fluted cookie cutter, stamp out 24 circles, each 2½ inches in diameter. Press them gently into the prepared pans, rerolling the trimmings as needed.

4. Brush the top edges of the pastry shells with a little of the egg glaze, then spoon in the filling.

5. Roll the reserved pie dough out thinly on a lightly floured surface. Stamp out 24 circles, each 2 inches in diameter, rerolling the trimmings as needed. Use a cookie cutter to cut hearts from each circle, some tiny, some bigger. Use the circles and bigger hearts as lids, pressing the edges together. Brush egg glaze over the pastry and sprinkle with superfine sugar.

6. Bake in the preheated oven for 15 minutes, or until golden. Let stand to cool in the pans for 10 minutes, then loosen with a blunt knife and transfer to a wire rack to cool. Whip the cream until it forms soft swirls, then fold in half of the lime rind and all of the confectioners' sugar. Sprinkle with the rest of the lime rind. Serve spoonfuls of the cream with the pies.

Deep South cherry pies

Makes: 24 mini muffin-size pies
Prep: 30 minutes
Cook: 15 minutes

a little butter, for greasing

2½ cups pitted and halved
cherries, plus extra to decorate

2 teaspoons cornstarch

3 tablespoons superfine or
granulated sugar

1 teaspoon vanilla extract

½ teaspoon ground cinnamon

⅔ quantity flaky pie dough
(see page 68) or 1 pound store-
bought rolled dough pie crust,
chilled

all-purpose flour, for dusting

1 egg yolk mixed with
1 tablespoon water, to glaze

2 tablespoons superfine or
granulated sugar mixed with a
large pinch ground cinnamon,
for sprinkling

*These are sure to evoke happy memories of childhood.
They're delicious served still hot from the oven with
whipped cream or a spoonful of vanilla ice cream.*

1. Preheat the oven to 350°F. Lightly grease two 12-cup mini muffin pans.

2. Put the pitted cherries in a mixing bowl and stir in the cornstarch,
sugar, vanilla extract, and cinnamon.

3. Roll two-thirds of the pie dough out thinly on a lightly floured surface.
Using a fluted cookie cutter, stamp out 24 circles, each 2½ inches in
diameter. Press them into the prepared pans, rerolling the trimmings
as needed.

4. Brush the top edges of the pastry shells with a little of the egg glaze,
then spoon in the filling.

5. Roll the reserved pie dough out thinly on a lightly floured surface. Stamp
out 24 circles, each 2 inches in diameter, rerolling the trimmings as needed.
Arrange these on top of the pies, pressing the edges together to seal. Brush
some egg glaze over the pastry. Use a cookie cutter to cut tiny hearts and
flowers from the remaining pie dough and arrange these on the lids. Brush
egg glaze over the decorations.

6. Bake in the preheated oven for 15 minutes, or until golden. Let stand
to cool in the pans for 10 minutes, then loosen with a blunt knife and
transfer to a wire rack to cool. Serve warm or cold, sprinkled with the
cinnamon mixture, on a plate decorated with extra cherries.

Peach and chocolate meringue pies

Makes: 6 muffin-size pies
Prep: 40 minutes
Cook: 22–25 minutes

What is there not to like? Crisp hazelnut pastry with a slightly tart peach filling that contrasts with a soft cloud of sweet meringue swirled with melted semisweet chocolate. You don't need to add anything, not even cream.

⅓ quantity hazelnut all-butter pie dough (see page 69) or 8 ounces store-bought rolled dough pie crust, chilled

all-purpose flour, for dusting

2 tablespoons butter, plus extra for greasing

2 peaches, peeled if liked, halved, pitted, and diced

2 ounces semisweet chocolate, coarsely chopped

2 egg whites

¼ cup superfine sugar

1. Lightly grease a six-cup muffin pan. Roll out the pie dough thinly on a lightly floured surface. Using a plain cookie cutter, stamp out six circles, each, 4 inches in diameter. Press them gently into the prepared pan, rerolling the trimmings as needed. Prick the bottom of each pastry shell with a fork, then chill in the refrigerator for 15 minutes. Preheat the oven to 375°F.

2. Line the pastry shells with squares of crumpled parchment paper and pie weights or dried beans. Bake in the preheated oven for 10 minutes. Remove the paper and weights and bake the pastry shells for an additional 2–3 minutes, until the bottom of the pastry is crisp and dry.

3. Meanwhile, melt the butter in a small skillet or saucepan, add the peaches, and cook gently for 5 minutes, stirring occasionally, until softened. Spoon the peaches into the pastry shells.

4. Put the chocolate in a heatproof bowl, set it over a saucepan of gently simmering water, and heat until melted. Whisk the egg whites in a large, clean mixing bowl until you have stiff, moist-looking peaks, then gradually whisk in the sugar, a teaspoon at a time, for another 1–2 minutes, or until the meringue is thick and glossy. Fold the melted chocolate into the meringue with just a couple of swirls of the spoon to create a marbled effect. Spoon into the pies.

5. Bake in the preheated oven for 5–7 minutes, or until the meringue peaks are golden and just cooked through. Let stand to cool in the pan for 10 minutes, then loosen with a blunt knife and transfer to a wire rack to cool. Serve warm.

Thanksgiving apple pies

Makes: 24 mini muffin-size pies
Prep: 35 minutes
Cook: 23–25 minutes

4 cups quartered, cored, peeled, and diced Pippin or other baking apples

2 tablespoons butter, plus extra for greasing

¼ cup superfine or granulated sugar, plus extra for sprinkling

⅓ cup golden raisins or raisins

grated rind of 1 lemon

3 tablespoons bourbon or brandy

1 quantity all-butter pie dough (see page 69) or 1½ pounds store-bought rolled dough pie crust, chilled

all-purpose flour, for dusting

milk, to glaze

whipped cream, to serve

These dainty, little deep pies have been personalized by adding an initial made from a tiny rope of pastry for each of your dinner guests; if you have a set of little alphabet cutters, then you may want to use them. If you prefer, bake the pies in advance and freeze them when cool, then warm through when needed.

1. Preheat the oven to 350°F. Lightly grease two 12-cup mini muffin pans.

2. Put the apples in a medium saucepan with the butter, sugar, golden raisins, and lemon rind. Cook, uncovered, over gentle heat, stirring from time to time, for 8–10 minutes, or until the apples have softened but still hold their shape. Add the bourbon and cook until just bubbling. Keeping it over the heat, set alight with a taper or long match, stand well back, and cook for a minute or so, until the flame subsides. Let the mixture cool.

3. Roll half of the pie dough out thinly on a lightly floured surface. Using a fluted cookie cutter, stamp out 24 circles, each 2½ inches in diameter. Press them gently into the prepared pans, rerolling the trimmings as needed.

4. Brush the top edges of the pastry shells with milk, then spoon in the filling, mounding it up high in the center.

5. Roll the reserved pie dough out thinly on a lightly floured surface. Stamp out 24 circles, the same size as before, rerolling the trimmings as needed. Arrange these on top of the pies, pressing the edges together well to seal. Brush milk over the pastry.

6. Shape tiny ropes from the remaining pastry into the initials of your dinner guests or family. Press them onto the pie tops, brush with a little extra milk, and sprinkle with sugar.

7. Bake in the preheated oven for 15 minutes, or until golden. Let stand to cool in the pans for 10 minutes, then loosen with a blunt knife and transfer to a wire rack to cool. Serve warm or cold, sprinkled with a little extra sugar, with spoonfuls of whipped cream.

Hot spiced pumpkin pies

Makes: 24 mini muffin-size pies
Prep: 30 minutes
Cook: 30 minutes

a little butter, for greasing

2 cups pumpkin puree (not pie filling) or 2 cups peeled, seeded, and diced butternut squash

¼ cup low-fat milk

2 eggs

3 tablespoons honey

1 teaspoon ground ginger

¼ teaspoon ground pumpkin pie spice

½ quantity all-butter pie dough (see page 69) or 12 ounces store-bought rolled dough pie crust, chilled

all-purpose flour, for dusting

milk, to glaze

superfine or granulated sugar, for sprinkling

These are always popular for Halloween. Serve them as they are or top with a spoonful of whipped cream flavored with a little honey or maple syrup.

1. Preheat the oven to 375°F. Lightly grease two 12-cup mini muffin pans.

2. If using the butternut squash, put it a steamer, cover, and set over a saucepan of gently simmering water. Steam for 15 minutes, or until tender. Puree in a blender or food processor until smooth and let cool slightly. For either the pumpkin puree or squash puree, blend the puree with the milk, then mix in the eggs, honey, ginger, and pumpkin pie spice.

3. Roll out the pie dough thinly on a lightly floured surface. Using a plain cookie cutter, stamp out 24 circles, each 2½ inches in diameter. Press them gently into the pan cups, rerolling the trimmings as needed. Squeeze any remaining trimmings together and reserve.

4. Brush the top edges of the pastry shells with milk, then spoon in the filling.

5. Roll the remaining pie dough trimmings out thinly on a lightly floured surface. Use a sharp knife to cut tiny leaves and mark on veins with the tip of the knife. Brush these with milk, arrange them over each pie, and sprinkle with a little sugar.

6. Bake in the preheated oven for 15 minutes, or until the leaves are golden and the filling is just set. Let stand to cool in the pans for 10 minutes, then loosen with a blunt knife and transfer to a wire rack to cool. Serve warm or

Christmas cranberry and orange pies

Makes: 12 mini muffin-size pies
Prep: 30 minutes
Cook: 30 minutes

Cranberries shouldn't be reserved just for sauce to go with the turkey; try them gently poached with star anise for a fragrant filling in an orange-scented pie crust. The secret to cooking cranberries is not to add sugar at first, but instead when the skins have softened. For a festive accompaniment, serve with whipped cream flavored with orange liqueur.

butter, for greasing

1¾ cups frozen cranberries

1 tablespoon cornstarch

3 tablespoons freshly squeezed orange juice

2 star anise

¼ cup superfine or granulated sugar, plus extra for sprinkling

⅓ quantity orange flaky pie dough (see pages 68–69) or 8 ounces store-bought rolled dough pie crust, chilled

all-purpose flour, for dusting

milk, to glaze

1. Preheat the oven to 350°F. Lightly grease a 12-cup mini muffin pan.

2. Put the still-frozen cranberries in a medium saucepan along with the cornstarch and orange juice. Add the star anise and cook, uncovered, over low heat, stirring from time to time, for 5 minutes, or until the cranberries have softened. Add the sugar and cook for an additional 5 minutes, then let stand to cool.

3. Roll out the pie dough thinly on a lightly floured surface. Using a fluted cookie cutter, stamp out 12 circles, each 2½ inches in diameter. Press them gently into the prepared pan, rerolling the trimmings as needed. Squeeze any remaining trimmings together and reserve.

4. Brush the top edges of the pastry shells with a little milk. Discard the star anise, then spoon in the filling.

5. Roll the remaining pie dough out thinly on a lightly floured surface. Using a fluted pastry wheel, cut thin strips of pastry. Arrange these over each pie and brush with a little milk. Sprinkle with a little sugar. Bake in the preheated oven for 20 minutes, covering with aluminum foil after 10 minutes if the tops are browning too quickly. Let stand to cool in the pan for 10 minutes, then loosen with a blunt knife and transfer to a wire rack to cool. Serve warm or cold.

Shaker lemon pies

Makes: 24 mini muffin-size pies
Prep: 40 minutes
Cook: 55 minutes

These are traditionally made with thin-skin Meyer lemons soaked for hours in sugar before baking, but because they can be difficult to find, ordinary lemons have been used here instead. To get around the increased bitterness, two are thinly sliced and poached in a sugar syrup, then mixed with extra grated lemon rind and juice for a tangy filling.

3½ lemons

1¼ cups superfine or granulated sugar, plus extra for sprinkling

¼ cup water

4 tablespoons butter, plus extra for greasing

3 eggs

⅔ quantity all-butter pie dough (see page 69) or 1 pound store-bought rolled dough pie crust, chilled

all-purpose flour, for dusting

egg white, to glaze

1. Lightly grease two 12-cup mini muffin pans. Thinly slice two of the lemons—you need 24 slices. Put them in a medium saucepan with ½ cup of the sugar and the water and stir. Cook, uncovered, over low heat, stirring from time to time, for 30 minutes, or until the slices are soft and translucent and just beginning to lose their color. Using a fork, scoop the slices out of the saucepan, draining off the syrup, and put them on a plate.

2. Preheat the oven to 350°F. Grate the rind and squeeze the juice from the remaining lemons. Add them to the syrup with the butter and remaining sugar. Heat gently, uncovered, until the butter is just melted.

3. Meanwhile, beat the eggs in a small bowl. Remove the pan from the heat and pour the eggs through a strainer into it, stirring well. Return to the heat and cook gently for 10 minutes, stirring frequently, or until the mixture has thickened and is like a preserves. Increase the heat, if needed, but keep a watchful eye; if it gets too hot, the eggs will curdle. Let stand to cool.

4. Roll half of the pie dough out thinly on a lightly floured surface. Using a fluted cookie cutter, stamp out 24 circles, each 2½ inches in diameter. Press them gently into the prepared pans, rerolling trimmings as needed.

5. Brush the top edges of the pastry shells with a little egg white, then spoon in the filling. Top each with a slice of candied lemon from step 1.

6. Roll the reserved pie dough out thinly on a lightly floured surface. Stamp out 24 circles, each 2 inches in diameter, rerolling the trimmings as needed. Press them onto the pie tops, pressing the edges together well.

7. Make four small cuts in the top of each pie, brush the pies with egg white, and sprinkle with sugar. Bake in the preheated oven for 15 minutes, or until golden. Let stand to cool in the pans for 10 minutes, then loosen with a blunt knife and transfer to a wire rack to cool. Serve warm or cold.

Lemon meringue pies

Makes: 12 muffin-size pies
Prep: 30 minutes
Cook: 18-22 minutes

1 stick butter, plus extra for greasing

2 tablespoons light corn syrup

2½ cups crushed graham crackers or plain cookies

grated rind and juice of 3 lemons

1 cup granulated sugar

⅓ cup cornstarch

3 eggs, separated

This all-time classic is loved by everyone, with its sharp, tangy lemon filling topped generously with piped or spooned meringue. These are made with a crumb crust.

1. Preheat the oven to 350°F. Lightly grease a 12-cup muffin pan.

2. Put the butter and syrup in a small saucepan and heat until the butter has just melted. Take the pan off the heat, stir in the cracker crumbs, then divide the mixture among the cups of the prepared pan. Press it firmly over the bottom and sides of the pan with the back of a teaspoon.

3. Line the crumb shells with parchment paper, fill with pie weights or dried beans, then bake them in the preheated oven for 8-10 minutes, or until slightly darker in color. Let stand to cool and harden in the pan for 10-15 minutes. Remove the paper and weights.

4. Put the lemon rind in a second, slightly larger saucepan. Make the juice up to 2 cups with cold water, then add this liquid to the rind and bring just to a boil. In a mixing bowl, stir together ¼ cup of the sugar, the cornstarch, and egg yolks until a thick paste has formed, then gradually stir in the boiling lemon juice until smooth.

5. Pour the liquid back into the saucepan and cook over medium heat, stirring continuously, for a few minutes, until it is thick and smooth. Spoon the filling into the cracker crumb shells.

6. For the topping, whisk the egg whites in a large, clean mixing bowl until they form stiff peaks, then gradually whisk in the remaining sugar, a teaspoon at a time, for another 1-2 minutes, or until the meringue is thick and glossy. Spoon or pipe the meringue on top of the pies.

7. Bake in the preheated oven for 10-12 minutes, or until the meringue peaks are golden and just cooked through. Let stand to cool and firm up in the pan, then loosen with a blunt knife and transfer to a plate.

S'more pies

Makes: 12 mini muffin-size pies
Prep: 20 minutes
Cook: 9–10 minutes

This summer camp favorite gets the grown-up treatment: mini crumb shells flavored with peanut butter, then filled with a rich chocolate cream and piled high with tiny marshmallows. They are great with coffee or hot chocolate at the end of a barbecue.

3 tablespoons butter, plus extra for greasing

1 tablespoon chunky peanut butter

¾ cup crushed graham crackers or plain cookies

4 ounces semisweet chocolate, coarsely chopped

1 tablespoon confectioners' sugar

⅓ cup heavy cream

¾ cup miniature marshmallows

1. Preheat the oven to 350°F. Grease a 12-cup mini muffin pan.

2. Put the butter in a small saucepan. Gently heat, uncovered, until it has melted. Take the saucepan off the heat and stir in the peanut butter, then the cracker crumbs. Divide among the cups of the prepared pan. Press it firmly over the bottom and sides of the pan with the back of a teaspoon.

3. Bake in the preheated oven for 6 minutes, or until slightly darker in color. Reshape the center, if needed, with the back of a spoon. Let stand to cool and harden in the pan for 10–15 minutes.

4. Meanwhile, put the chocolate in a heatproof bowl, set the bowl over a saucepan of gently simmering water, and heat until melted. Add the sugar and gradually stir in the cream until smooth. Preheat the broiler to medium.

5. Spoon the filling into the shells. Sprinkle the mini marshmallows over the top and press them lightly into the chocolate so they don't roll off.

6. Broil for 3–4 minutes, or until the marshmallows have softened and are just beginning to color. Let stand to cool in the pan for 30 minutes, then loosen with a blunt knife and carefully lift out of the pan. Serve.

Blueberry tarts

Makes: 24 mini muffin-size pies
Prep: 25 minutes
Cook: 17–18 minutes

2 cups blueberries

2 teaspoons cornstarch

¼ cup superfine or granulated sugar

4 teaspoons water

½ cup all-purpose flour, plus extra for dusting

grated rind of 1 lemon

3 tablespoons butter, diced, plus extra for greasing

½ quantity all-butter pie dough (see page 69) or 12 ounces store-bought rolled dough pie crust, chilled

Crisp, dainty pies with a moist blueberry filling and a buttery streusel crumb top. Serve while still warm, with good vanilla ice cream.

1. Preheat the oven to 375°F. Lightly grease two 12-cup mini muffin pans.

2. Put half of the blueberries in a small saucepan with the cornstarch, half of the superfine sugar, and the water. Cook, uncovered, over medium heat, stirring continuously, for 2–3 minutes, or until the juices begin to run and the sauce thickens. Take the pan off the heat and add the remaining blueberries.

3. For the streusel, put the flour, lemon rind, butter, and remaining sugar in a medium mixing bowl. Toss together, then lift the mixture and rub it through your fingers and thumbs until it looks like fine bread crumbs.

4. Roll out the pie dough thinly on a lightly floured surface. Using a fluted cookie cutter, stamp out 24 circles, each 2½ inches in diameter. Press them into the prepared pans, rerolling the trimmings as needed. Spoon the blueberry filling into the pastry shells, then sprinkle the tops of the tarts with the streusel mixture.

5. Bake in the preheated oven for 15 minutes, or until the topping is pale gold. Let stand to cool in the pans for 10 minutes, then loosen with a blunt knife and transfer to a wire rack to cool.

2

3

4

Orchard tarts

Makes: 6 muffin-size pies
Prep: 45 minutes
Cook: 32–33 minutes

a little butter, for greasing

⅓ quantity all-butter pie dough
(see page 69) or 8 ounces store-
bought rolled dough pie crust,
chilled

all-purpose flour, for dusting

1 cup quartered, cored, peeled,
and diced pears

1⅓ cups quartered, cored, peeled,
and diced Pippin or other baking
apples

3 ripe red plums, halved, pitted,
and diced

2 tablespoons superfine or
granulated sugar

1 tablespoon water

1 tablespoon sunflower oil

1 tablespoon honey

¼ cup rolled oats

1 tablespoon sesame seeds

2 tablespoons sunflower seeds

2 tablespoons pumpkin seeds

2 tablespoons coarsely chopped
hazelnuts

Apple pies with a twist — they are sprinkled with homemade granola (a mix of oats, seeds, and nuts). Mix and match the topping ingredients to suit your pantry; try barley flakes, slivered almonds, chopped macadamia nuts, or pumpkin seeds.

1. Lightly grease a six-cup muffin pan. Roll out the pie dough thinly on a lightly floured surface. Using a plain cookie cutter, stamp out six circles, each 4 inches in diameter. Press them gently into the prepared pan, rerolling the trimmings as needed. Prick the bottom of each with a fork, then chill in the refrigerator for 15 minutes. Preheat the oven to 375°F.

2. Line the pastry shells with squares of crumpled parchment paper and pie weights or dried beans. Bake in the preheated oven for 10 minutes. Remove the paper and weights and bake the pastry shells for an additional 2–3 minutes, or until the bottom of the pastry is crisp and dry. Turn the oven down to 350°F.

3. Put all the fruit, sugar, and water in a medium saucepan. Cover and cook over gentle heat, stirring, for 5 minutes, or until the fruit has just softened. Meanwhile, for the granola, warm the oil and honey in a skillet. Stir in the oats, seeds, and hazelnuts and set aside. Spoon the fruit into the pastry shells, then sprinkle the granola on top.

4. Bake in the preheated oven for 20 minutes, covering with aluminum foil after 10 minutes if the granola is browning too quickly. Let stand to cool in the pan for 10 minutes, then loosen with a blunt knife and transfer to a wire rack to cool. Serve warm.

Caramelized apple tarts

Makes: 12 muffin-size pies
Prep: 45 minutes
Cook: 32–36 minutes

These French-inspired tarts are filled with a tangy apple and lemon custard, then topped with wafer-thin sliced apples and glazed with confectioners' sugar. They can be difficult to remove from the pan because the sugar glaze makes them sticky, so be extra careful.

⅔ quantity flaky pie dough (see page 68) or 1 pound store-bought rolled dough pie crust, chilled

all-purpose flour, for dusting

5 Granny Smith or other baking apples, quartered, cored, and peeled

½ cup superfine or granulated sugar

finely grated rind and juice of 1 lemon

2 eggs

1 tablespoon butter, plus extra for greasing

3 tablespoons confectioners' sugar, sifted

1. Lightly grease a 12-cup muffin pan. Roll out the pie dough thinly on a lightly floured surface. Using a plain cookie cutter, stamp out 12 circles, each 4 inches in diameter. Press them gently into the prepared pan, rerolling the trimmings as needed. Prick the bottom of each with a fork, then chill in the refrigerator for 15 minutes. Preheat the oven to 375°F.

2. Line the pastry shells with squares of crumpled parchment paper and pie weights or dried beans. Bake in the preheated oven for 10 minutes. Remove the paper and weights and cook the pastry shells for an additional 2–3 minutes, or until the bottom of the pastry is crisp and dry. Turn the oven down to 350°F.

3. Coarsely grate eight of the apple quarters into a mixing bowl. Add two-thirds of the superfine sugar, all the lemon rind and juice, and the eggs and beat together. Spoon the filling into the pastry shells.

4. Thinly slice the remaining apples and arrange them overlapping on top of the pies. Sprinkle with the remaining superfine sugar and then dot the pies with the butter.

5. Bake in the preheated oven for 20–25 minutes, or until the filling is set and the sliced apples are browned around the edges.

6. Dust with the confectioners' sugar and return the pies to the oven for 5 minutes, or until the sugar has caramelized. Let stand to cool in the pan for 15 minutes, then loosen with a blunt knife and transfer to a wire rack to cool. Serve warm or cold.

Mississippi mud pies

Makes: 6 muffin-size pies
Prep: 30 minutes
Cook: 12–13 minutes

a little butter, for greasing

⅓ quantity chocolate or hazelnut
pie dough (see pages 68–69)
or 8 ounces store-bought rolled
dough pie crust, chilled

all-purpose flour, for dusting

4 ounces semisweet chocolate,
coarsely chopped

¼ cup confectioners' sugar

½ cup low-fat milk

1 egg

1 cup heavy cream

1 teaspoon vanilla extract

white and semisweet chocolate
curls, to decorate

A dark, rich, almost trufflelike chocolate layer covered in an even darker, crisp chocolate pastry, then topped with soft swirls of Chantilly cream.

1. Lightly grease a six-cup muffin pan. Roll out the pie dough thinly on a lightly floured surface. Using a plain cookie cutter, stamp out six circles, each 4 inches in diameter. Press them gently into the prepared pan, rerolling the trimmings as needed. Prick the bottom of each with a fork, then chill in the refrigerator for 15 minutes. Preheat the oven to 375°F.

2. Line the pastry shells with squares of crumpled parchment paper and pie weights or dried beans. Bake in the preheated oven for 10 minutes. Remove the paper and weights and bake the pastry shells for an additional 2–3 minutes, or until the bottom of the pastry is crisp and dry.

3. Meanwhile, put the semisweet chocolate in a heatproof bowl, set the bowl over a saucepan of gently simmering water, and heat until melted. Beat together 2 tablespoons of the sugar, the milk, and the egg in a small bowl. Remove the bowl of chocolate from the heat and gradually stir in the milk mixture until smooth. Pour the filling into the pastry shells and let stand to cool. Transfer the pies to the refrigerator for 2 hours, or until the filling has set.

4. Whip the cream with the remaining confectioners' sugar and the vanilla until it forms soft folds. Loosen the pastry shells with a blunt knife and lift them onto a plate. Spoon the cream over the top and decorate with the chocolate curls.

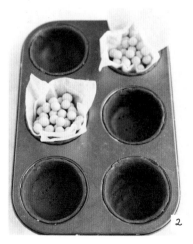

Chocolate and pecan tarts

Makes: 24 mini muffin-size pies
Prep: 25 minutes
Cook: 20 minutes

½ cup light corn syrup

⅓ cup packed light brown sugar

2 tablespoons butter, plus extra
for greasing

4 ounces semisweet
chocolate, coarsely chopped

½ quantity all-butter cinnamon
pie dough (see page 69)
or 12 ounces prepared
all-butter pie dough, chilled

all-purpose flour, for dusting

1 egg, beaten

1 egg yolk

1 cup pecans

These tarts freeze well if packed into a plastic container. Once defrosted, dust with confectioners' sugar and drizzle with melted chocolate before serving. Alternatively, warm them in the oven and serve with whipped cream flavored with ground cinnamon or Greek yogurt and honey.

1. Preheat the oven to 350°F. Lightly grease two 12-cup mini muffin pans.

2. Put the syrup, sugar, and butter in a small saucepan. Heat gently, uncovered, stirring from time to time, until the butter has just melted. Add half the chocolate and then stir until it too has melted. Let stand to cool slightly.

3. Roll out the pie dough thinly on a lightly floured surface. Using a fluted cookie cutter, stamp out 24 circles, each 2½ inches in diameter. Press them gently into the prepared pans, rerolling the trimmings as needed.

4. Stir the egg and egg yolk into the cooled chocolate mixture until smooth, then spoon this filling into the pastry shells. Decorate the top of each pie with two pecans.

5. Bake in the preheated oven for 20 minutes, or until the filling has set, covering with aluminum foil after 10 minutes if the nuts are browning too quickly. Let stand to cool in the pans for 10 minutes, then loosen with a blunt knife and transfer to a wire rack to cool.

6. For the decoration, put the remaining chocolate in a heatproof bowl, set the bowl over a saucepan of gently simmering water, and heat until melted. Spoon the chocolate into a paper pastry bag, snip off the tip, and pipe zigzag lines of melted chocolate over the pies, or drizzle the chocolate from a teaspoon. Let the pies stand to set for 10 minutes, then arrange on a serving plate.

Pistachio and almond tarts

Makes: 12 mini muffin-size pies
Prep: 20 minutes
Cook: 15 minutes

⅓ quantity flaky pie dough (see page 68) or 8 ounces store-bought rolled dough pie crust, chilled

all-purpose flour, for dusting

3½ tablespoons butter, softened, plus extra for greasing

¼ cup superfine sugar

1 egg yolk

½ cup ground almonds (almond meal)

a few drops of almond extract or orange flower water

1½ tablespoons slivered almonds

1 tablespoon thinly sliced pistachio nuts

a little confectioners' sugar, sifted, to decorate

A true French frangipane is made with only almonds, but a mixture of pretty green-tinged, sliced pistachios and ground and slivered almonds makes these luxurious mini pies.

1. Lightly grease a 12-cup mini muffin pan. Preheat the oven to 350°F.

2. Roll out the pie dough thinly on a lightly floured surface. Using a fluted cookie cutter, stamp out 12 circles, each 2½ inches in diameter. Press them gently into the prepared pan, rerolling the trimmings as needed.

3. Meanwhile, put the butter and superfine sugar in a mixing bowl and beat together until light and fluffy. Beat in the egg yolk, then the ground almonds. Flavor with a little almond extract or orange flower water.

4. Spoon the frangipane into the pastry shells.

5. Sprinkle the slivered almonds and sliced pistachios over the top and press them lightly into the filling.

6. Bake in the preheated oven for 15 minutes, or until the almonds are golden. Let stand to cool in the pan for 10 minutes, then loosen with a blunt knife and transfer to a wire rack to cool. Serve warm or cold, dusted with sifted confectioners' sugar.

Coffee tarts

Makes: 12 muffin-size pies
Prep: 40 minutes
Cook: 27–33 minutes

Dark, rich, and not overly sweet. Bite through a crisp, buttery pastry shell to a coffee and semisweet chocolate custard, topped with whipped cream that is flavored with coffee cream liqueur. Delicious served with a cup of strong black coffee.

a little butter, for greasing

⅔ quantity all-butter pie dough (see page 69) or 1 pound store-bought rolled dough pie crust, chilled

all-purpose flour, for dusting

1 cup low-fat milk

4 ounces semisweet chocolate, coarsely chopped

2 teaspoons instant coffee powder or granules

2 tablespoons superfine or granulated sugar

2 eggs

2 egg yolks

DECORATION

1 cup heavy cream

2 tablespoons confectioners' sugar

2 tablespoons coffee cream liqueur

1½ teaspoons instant coffee dissolved in 1 teaspoon boiling water

white chocolate curls, to decorate

sifted unsweetened cocoa powder, to decorate

1. Lightly grease a 12-cup muffin pan. Roll out the pie dough thinly on a lightly floured surface. Using a plain cookie cutter, stamp out 12 circles, each 4 inches in diameter. Press them gently into the prepared pan, rerolling the trimmings as needed. Prick the bottom of each with a fork, then chill for 15 minutes. Preheat the oven to 375°F.

2. Line the pastry shells with squares of crumpled parchment paper and pie weights or dried beans. Bake in the preheated oven for 10 minutes. Remove the paper and weights and bake the pastry shells for an additional 2–3 minutes, or until the bottom of the pastry is crisp. Turn the oven down to 325°F. Meanwhile, bring the milk just to a boil in a small saucepan. Add the chocolate, coffee, and superfine sugar and let stand, off the heat, until the chocolate has melted.

3. Beat the eggs and yolks in a mixing bowl, then gradually whisk in the warm milk mixture until smooth. Pour the custard into the pastry shells.

4. Bake in the preheated oven for 15–20 minutes, or until just set. Let stand to cool in the pan for 10 minutes, then loosen with a blunt knife and transfer to a wire rack. Whip the cream in a bowl until it forms soft swirls. Add the sugar, then whisk in the liqueur and coffee until thick. Spoon over the pies, then decorate with white chocolate curls and a dusting of cocoa.

Cherry cream pies

Makes: 12 muffin-size pies
Prep: 30 minutes
Cook: 25–30 minutes

These cream cheese pies are perfect for a special summer picnic, although you may need to pack them with a little crumpled aluminum foil or paper towels to protect them from being banged about. Serve with a spoonful of whipped cream flavored with a little sugar and vanilla.

a little butter, for greasing

1¼ cups mascarpone cheese

2 teaspoons all-purpose flour, plus extra for dusting

½ cup superfine or granulated sugar, plus extra for sprinkling

2 eggs

⅔ cup plain yogurt

1 teaspoon vanilla extract

⅔ quantity all-butter pie dough (see page 69) or 1 pound store-bought rolled dough pie crust, chilled

milk, to glaze

36 fresh or canned cherries, pitted and drained well

1. Lightly grease a 12-cup muffin pan. Preheat the oven to 350°F.

2. Spoon the mascarpone cheese into a mixing bowl and add the flour, sugar, eggs, yogurt, and vanilla. Beat with a wooden spoon or an electric handheld mixer until just mixed.

3. Roll out the pie dough thinly on a lightly floured surface. Using a plain cookie cutter, stamp out 12 circles, each 4 inches in diameter. Press them gently into the prepared pan, rerolling the trimmings as needed and reserving any remaining pastry. Brush the top edges of the pastry shells with some of the milk glaze and spoon in the filling. Add three cherries to each pie.

4. Roll the reserved pie dough out thinly on a lightly floured surface. Cut strips about ½ inch wide. Arrange four strips over each pie to make a lattice, pressing the edges together well to seal, then brush milk over the pastry and sprinkle with a little sugar.

5. Bake in the preheated oven for 25–30 minutes, or until the lattice is golden and the filling is just set. Let stand to cool in the pan for 10 minutes, then loosen with a blunt knife and transfer to a wire rack to cool. Serve at room temperature.

Key lime pies

Makes: 24 mini muffin-size pies
Prep: 15 minutes
Cook: 6–8 minutes

¼ cup light corn syrup

5 tablespoons butter, plus extra for greasing

1½ cups crushed graham crackers or plain cookies

⅔ cup heavy cream

grated rind of 2 limes

⅔ cup canned sweetened condensed milk

¼ cup freshly squeezed lime juice (about 2 limes)

extra lime zest, to decorate

These superspeedy mini pies are filled with a luscious no-bake citrusy cream sweetened with condensed milk. They're great to make with kids.

1. Preheat the oven to 350°F. Lightly grease two 12-cup mini muffin pans.

2. Put the syrup and butter in a small saucepan. Heat gently, uncovered, stirring, until the butter has just melted. Take the saucepan off the heat and stir in the cracker crumbs. Divide the mixture among the cups of the prepared pans. Press it firmly over the bottom and sides of the pans with the back of a teaspoon.

3. Bake in the preheated oven for 6 minutes, or until slightly darker in color. Reshape the center, if needed, with the back of a spoon. Let stand to cool and harden in the pans for 10–15 minutes.

4. Meanwhile, pour the cream into a bowl, add the lime rind, and beat until it is beginning to thicken. Gradually beat in the condensed milk, then the lime juice, beating for another few minutes until it has thickened.

5. Pipe or spoon the lime cream into the pie shells. Chill for 30 minutes, or longer if you have time. Loosen the pies with a blunt knife and lift them carefully out of the pans. Decorate with lime zest curls.

Maple cream pies with orange

Makes: 12 muffin-size pies
Prep: 45 minutes
Cook: 37–38 minutes

Delicately flavored creamy pies with a hint of maple and orange rind. Delicious served at room temperature, with extra orange segments and a drizzle of maple syrup.

a little butter, for greasing

⅔ quantity all-butter pie dough (see page 69) or 1 pound store-bought rolled dough pie crust, chilled

all-purpose flour, for dusting

1 cup heavy cream

½ cup maple syrup

2 eggs

2 egg yolks

grated rind of 1 orange

TO SERVE

3 oranges, peeled and segmented

3 tablespoons maple syrup

1. Lightly grease a 12-cup muffin pan. Roll out the pie dough thinly on a lightly floured surface. Using a fluted cookie cutter, stamp out 12 circles, each 4 inches in diameter. Press them gently into the prepared pan, rerolling the trimmings as needed. Prick the bottom of each with a fork, then chill in the refrigerator for 15 minutes. Preheat the oven to 375°F.

2. Line the pastry shells with squares of crumpled parchment paper and pie weights or dried beans. Bake in the preheated oven for 10 minutes. Remove the paper and weights and cook the pastry shells for an additional 2–3 minutes, or until the bottom of the pastry is crisp and dry. Turn the oven down to 325°F.

3. Beat together the cream, syrup, eggs, egg yolks, and most of the orange rind in a small bowl. Pour this filling into the pastry shells.

4. Bake in the preheated oven for 25 minutes, or until the custard is set. Let stand to cool in the pans for 10 minutes, then loosen with a blunt knife and transfer to a serving plate.

5. Serve topped with extra orange segments, a sprinkling of the remaining grated orange rind, and a drizzle of maple syrup.

Honey, walnut, and ricotta pies

Makes: 24 mini muffin-size pies
Prep: 45 minutes
Cook: 25 minutes

Made here with a crisp, rich, all-butter pie dough, but these would also taste great with cinnamon flaky pie dough. It's the perfect pie for those who don't have a sweet tooth. Undecorated pies will keep in the refrigerator for two to three days.

a little butter, for greasing

a little olive oil, for greasing

½ quantity all-butter pie dough (see page 69) or 12 ounces store-bought rolled dough pie crust, chilled

all-purpose flour, for dusting

1 cup walnut pieces

1 cup ricotta cheese

2 egg yolks

⅓ cup orange blossom honey

a large pinch of ground cinnamon

½ cup granulated sugar

1 tablespoon water

1 cup Greek yogurt, to serve

1. Lightly grease two 12-cup mini muffin pans and oil a baking sheet. Preheat the oven to 350°F.

2. Roll out the pie dough thinly on a lightly floured surface. Using a fluted cookie cutter, stamp out 24 circles, each 2½ inches in diameter. Press them gently into the prepared pans, rerolling the trimmings as needed.

3. Lightly toast half of the walnut pieces in a dry nonstick skillet. Let them cool, then coarsely chop them.

4. Lightly beat together the ricotta, egg yolks, ¼ cup of the honey, and the cinnamon in a mixing bowl until just mixed. Stir in the toasted walnuts. Spoon the filling into the pastry shells.

5. Bake in the preheated oven for 20 minutes, or until the filling is golden brown. Let stand in the pan for 10 minutes to cool.

6. Meanwhile, for the praline, put the sugar, remaining 1 tablespoon of honey, and the water into the skillet and heat gently without stirring until the sugar has dissolved. Tilt the pan to mix any remaining grains of sugar into the syrup. Add the remaining walnuts and cook over medium heat, again without stirring, for about 5 minutes, or until the syrup turns a rich golden brown. Keep a watchful eye on the syrup because it will suddenly begin to change color, darkening first around the edges. Tilt the pan to mix, if needed, then quickly pour the praline onto the prepared baking sheet and let cool and harden.

7. Loosen the pies with a blunt knife and transfer them to a plate. Just before serving, top them with spoonfuls of yogurt. Loosen the praline from the baking sheet with a knife, then break or cut it into thin shards and press pieces of it into the yogurt.

Coconut cream pies

Makes: 12 muffin-size pies
Prep: 40 minutes
Cook: 8–10 minutes

An all-American favorite made with a coconut filling and topped with vanilla cream. Ginger fans could try a little chopped candied preserved ginger in the cream instead of the vanilla flavoring.

2 tablespoons light corn syrup

1 stick butter, plus extra for greasing

2½ cups crushed gingersnaps or graham crackers

1 cup dry unsweetened flaked coconut

½ cup boiling water

¼ cup superfine or granulated sugar

3 tablespoons cornstarch

3 tablespoons all-purpose flour

2 egg yolks

1¼ cups milk

grated rind of 1 lime

1¼ cups heavy cream

1 teaspoon vanilla extract

2 tablespoons confectioners' sugar

toasted coconut curls or dry shredded coconut

1. Preheat the oven to 350°F. Lightly grease a 12-cup muffin pan.

2. Put the syrup and butter in a small saucepan. Heat gently, uncovered, stirring, until the butter has just melted. Remove the saucepan from the heat and stir in the cookie crumbs. Divide the mixture among the cups of the prepared pan. Press it firmly over the bottom and sides of the pan with the back of a teaspoon.

3. Line the crumb shells with parchment paper and pie weights or dried beans, then bake them in the preheated oven for 8–10 minutes, or until slightly darker in color. Let stand to cool and harden in the pan for 10–15 minutes. Remove the paper and weights.

4. Put the coconut into a mixing bowl and pour in the boiling water. Let stand for 10 minutes. Put the superfine sugar, cornstarch, all-purpose flour, and egg yolks in a separate mixing bowl and beat together.

5. Pour the milk into a small saucepan, bring just to a boil, then gradually whisk it into the egg yolk mixture until smooth. Return the milk mixture to the saucepan and cook over medium heat, whisking, until thick. The sauce will suddenly thicken, and as it does, you may find it easier to turn the heat all the way down to low so that you can whisk out any lumps quickly. Stir in the soaked coconut and the lime rind, cover the surface with wetted parchment paper, and let cool.

6. Loosen the pie shells with a blunt knife and carefully lift out of the pan. Spoon in the coconut filling.

7. Whip the cream until it just forms soft swirls, then fold in the vanilla extract and confectioners' sugar. Spoon the cream over the tops of the pies, then decorate with coconut curls or dry coconut.

Mini Desserts

Cooking techniques

Freezing

If you are freezing desserts served in glasses, choose plastic glasses. Arrange the desserts on a baking sheet or in a plastic container and freeze them uncovered until firm, then cover with plastic wrap or the plastic container lid, seal, and label. Use within six weeks. Defrost desserts in the refrigerator overnight or at room temperature for 2 hours, then transfer to the refrigerator. If the desserts have been frozen, do not return any leftovers to the freezer.

Gelatin

To use powdered gelatin, scoop it into a measuring spoon so the powder is level with the spoon, then sprinkle it over cold water in a small, heatproof bowl. If specks remain on the surface of the water, gently stir them in, using a spoon. Let the gelatin soak for 5 minutes (it forms a spongelike mixture), then stand the bowl in a small saucepan and pour water into the pan halfway up the sides of the bowl. Gently simmer the water for 5 minutes, until the gelatin melts and you have a clear, amber liquid. If it gets hot, let it cool for a few minutes. Trickle the gelatin into your wine, juice, or cream, then pour the mixture into serving dishes (if the dessert has sliced fruit, which may float, let the gelatin partly set before transferring it to the serving dishes). Chill in the refrigerator for 3–4 hours.

To invert the dessert, dip a metal mold into just-boiled water for 2 seconds (longer if it is silicone), then loosen the top of the dessert with your fingertips and invert the mold onto a serving plate. Holding the mold and plate, give a quick jerk, remove the mold, and clean the dish with paper towels. Serve within 30 minutes.

Caramel

The secret to caramel is to avoid stirring the sugar as it dissolves, because this can make it crystallize. Heat the sugar and water gently in a heavy saucepan, tilting it from time to time. Once the sugar has dissolved, boil rapidly for 4–5 minutes; the syrup will color around the edges and then will burn easily, so do not leave the pan unattended. Tilt the pan gently to encourage even coloring. When browned remove from the heat.

Meringues

Always use a clean, dry bowl and whisk or beaters. Whisk the egg whites until they form stiff, moist-looking peaks, then tilt the bowl; they won't move if they are ready. Gradually whisk in the sugar, a teaspoonful at a time, then continue to whisk for 1–2 minutes after it has been added to make the mixture smooth, thickened, and glossy. Spoon or pipe onto baking sheets lined with nonstick parchment paper and bake in a low oven, as specified in the recipe, until the meringues are crisp and can be lifted easily off the paper. If they are sticky on the bottom, cook for a few minutes longer, then try again. Cooled, unfilled meringues will keep in a cool place in a cookie jar layered with parchment paper for three to four days.

Decorating techniques

Chocolate curls

Spread just-melted chocolate over a marble pastry board or cheese board in an even layer no less than ¼-inch thick. Let stand in a cool place to set. To make the curls, draw a long chef's knife across the chocolate at a 45-degree angle in a seesaw action to shave the chocolate into curls. For two-tone chocolate caraque, spread a band of melted white chocolate on the marble, let set for 5 minutes, then spread a band of melted dark chocolate onto it, butting up to the white chocolate and making sure that the level of the chocolate is the same for both types. Let stand to set, then shave into curls as above.

For speedy chocolate curls, turn a block of chocolate over so that the smooth underside is uppermost, then place the block on a cutting board and run a vegetable peeler firmly over the surface so that the blade is at a slight angle to the chocolate. The size of the curl that you make will depend on the temperature of the chocolate and the amount of fat it contains. If the chocolate is cold, the curls will be tiny, so soften it in the microwave at full power for 10 seconds (if the bar is large or the chocolate is dark, you may need to give it a second burst in the microwave). The fewer cocoa solids the chocolate contains, the easier it will be to shape, so white and milk chocolate will make larger curls than dark chocolate.

Piped chocolate

Spoon melted chocolate into a small nonstick parchment paper pastry bag (see page 10), roll down the top to enclose the chocolate, then snip a little off the tip of the bag. There is no need to add a piping tip. Pipe shapes, such as leaves, flowers, butterflies, initials, and hearts, over nonstick parchment paper freehand, or draw them on a second sheet of paper, using a black pen, then slide it under the top sheet before piping. Fill in the shapes with extra piped squiggles of chocolate or flood the center to fill it completely.

Colored chocolate

Melted white chocolate can be colored with the tiniest amount of liquid food coloring and can make an eye-catching decoration piped over a layer of dark chocolate.

Sugar decorations

Ready-to-use fondant can be left white or colored with paste or gel food colorings before being shaped. Don't use liquid food colorings, because these will make the fondant sticky and difficult to roll out. Paste or gel colors can be bought from some large supermarkets, specialty cook shops, or online in a wide variety of colors. Apply the coloring on the end of a toothpick to the fondant and use sparingly. Knead the coloring in, then roll out the fondant thinly and stamp out stars, holly leaves, snowflakes, or tiny hearts or flowers, using cutters. (Look out for mini plunger flower cutters, because these can be depressed into a small circle of foam for a curved flower effect). Let the decorations dry at room temperature on a baking sheet lined with nonstick parchment paper, then store them in a small plastic container, interleaved with extra paper, for up to two months. You can also buy prepared sugar flowers or choose from a range of edible glitter, sugar strands, or tiny shapes from supermarkets or specialty suppliers.

Natural flower decorations

Tiny flowers can add a delicate finishing touch to a miniature dessert, but first make sure that they are edible. Choose from tiny viola or pansy flowers in a mix of colors to borage, violet, little rose petals, herb flowers or tiny mint leaves. Brush petals or leaves lightly with a little beaten egg white, then sprinkle with superfine sugar and let dry on a baking sheet lined with nonstick parchment paper for an hour. Use immediately.

Citrus curls

Pare away the rind from lemons, oranges, or limes with a zester (a small metal-topped tool with a row of holes punched in the top). Dust the curls with a little superfine sugar and sprinkle them over mousses or ice creams. For larger, corkscrew-type curls, remove the citrus peel in single, slightly larger strips with a canelle or paring knife, then twist each strip tightly around a toothpick, let stand for a minute, slide the toothpick out, and hang the corkscrew curl over the edge of the serving dish.

Caramel shards

Just-cooked caramel can be drizzled over nonstick parchment paper, then left to cool and harden. When ready to serve, break it into shards or chop it into small pieces. For extra interest, you can also add chopped or slivered nuts to the caramel before it hardens.

Blueberry and maple syrup pancakes

Makes: 30
Prep: 20 minutes
Cook: 10–15 minutes

Popular with diners of all ages, these bite-size pancakes take only a few minutes to prepare — which is just as well, because chances are they will disappear as soon as they are cooked.

1½ cups all-purpose flour

1 teaspoon baking powder

½ teaspoon baking soda

1 tablespoon granulated sugar

2 eggs, separated

finely grated rind of 1 lemon and juice of ½ lemon

1 cup milk

¾ cup blueberries

sunflower oil, for frying

maple syrup, to serve

crème fraîche or whipped cream, to serve (optional)

1. Put the flour, baking powder, and baking soda into a mixing bowl, then stir in the sugar. Whisk the egg whites in a separate large, clean mixing bowl until you have soft peaks.

2. Add the egg yolks, lemon rind, and lemon juice to the flour, then gradually whisk in the milk until smooth. Fold in a spoonful of the whisked egg whites, then add the rest and fold in gently. Sprinkle the blueberries into the bowl, then gently fold them in.

3. Pour a little oil into a large skillet, then place it over medium heat. When it's hot, drop tablespoonfuls of the blueberry batter into the skillet, leaving a little space between the pancakes. Cook for 2–3 minutes, until bubbles appear on the surface of the pancakes and the undersides are golden. Turn the pancakes over and cook the second side for 1–2 minutes, until golden.

4. Remove the pancakes from the skillet, using a spatula, and keep them hot in a clean dish towel. Cook the remaining blueberry batter in batches of ten pancakes at a time, until all the mixture is cooked, oiling the skillet as needed.

5. Transfer the pancakes to small dessert plates, serving four to five pancakes per serving. Drizzle a little maple syrup over them and serve extra syrup in a small pitcher. Top the pancakes with teaspoonfuls of crème fraîche, if desired.

Berry and oat crisps

Makes: 8
Prep: 20 minutes
Cook: 20 minutes

These comforting little desserts are always a great hit. If you prefer, make double the amount of the crumb topping and store it in the freezer, then use it at a later date and bake from frozen.

7 red plums (about 1 pound), halved, pitted, and diced

1 cup raspberries

2 tablespoons packed light brown sugar

3 tablespoons water

custard or heavy cream, to serve

TOPPING

¾ cup all-purpose flour

¼ cup rolled oats

½ cup barley flakes

3 tablespoons packed light brown sugar

3 tablespoons unsalted butter, chilled and diced

1. Preheat the oven to 350°F. Put the plums, raspberries, sugar, and water into a heavy saucepan. Cover and simmer for 5 minutes, or until the fruit has softened.

2. For the topping, put the flour, rolled oats, barley flakes, and sugar into a mixing bowl and stir. Rub in the butter, using your fingertips, until the mixture resembles fine crumbs.

3. Spoon the fruit mixture into eight ⅔-cup metal molds and stand them on a baking sheet. Sprinkle the topping on top.

4. Bake in the preheated oven for 15 minutes, or until golden. Let the crisps cool for 5–10 minutes, then serve topped with small spoonfuls of custard or cream.

Cinnamon and apple fritters with blackberry sauce

Makes: 30
Prep: 30 minutes
Cook: 20–35 minutes

A retro dessert that uses staple ingredients. It's a good way to make the most of blackberries you have in the freezer. Alternatively, use whatever frozen berries you have on hand — raspberries or blueberries would work well.

8 small apples, such as Pippin

1 cup blackberries

½ cup water

⅓ cup granulated sugar

1¼ cups all-purpose flour

a large pinch of ground cinnamon

1 egg, separated

⅔ cup milk

4 cups sunflower oil

1. For the sauce, quarter, core, peel, and dice two of the apples, then put them into a heavy saucepan. Add the blackberries, water, and a tablespoon of the sugar. Cover and simmer for 5–10 minutes, or until the apples have softened. Puree until smooth, using an immersion blender, then press through a strainer into a serving bowl to remove the seeds. Cover with plastic wrap and set aside.

2. Peel and core the remaining apples, cut them into thin rings, then put them in a plastic bag with ⅓ cup of the flour. Seal the bag, then shake to thinly coat the apples with the flour.

3. Put the remaining flour into a mixing bowl. Stir in a tablespoon of the sugar, the cinnamon, and the egg yolk. Gradually whisk in the milk until smooth.

4. Whisk the egg white in a separate large, clean mixing bowl until you have soft peaks. Fold it into the flour mixture.

5. Pour the oil into a saucepan, making sure that it is filled no more than halfway. Heat to 325°F on a candy thermometer, or until bubbles form when a little batter is dropped into the oil. Line a plate with paper towels.

6. Shake any excess flour from the apple slices, then dip them into the batter and remove them, using two forks. Drain off the excess batter, then carefully add four or five apple slices to the hot oil and cook for 2–3 minutes, or until golden. Lift out of the oil with a draining spoon, then transfer to the lined plate and let drain while you cook the remaining apples in batches of this size.

7. Sprinkle the remaining sugar over the fritters and serve with the blackberry sauce for dipping.

Hot orange soufflés with chocolate and orange sauce

Makes: 12
Prep: 25 minutes
Cook: 20–25 minutes

Serving hot soufflés adds a touch of suspense to any meal because they puff up dramatically in the oven but can fall just as quickly. Get your dinner guests ready and waiting, dust the tops of the soufflés with a speedy flourish of confectioners' sugar, then serve, hopefully to applause.

2 tablespoons unsalted butter, for greasing

½ cup superfine sugar, plus 2 tablespoons for sprinkling

3 eggs, separated, plus 1 extra egg white

⅓ cup all-purpose flour

1 cup milk

finely grated rind of 1 large orange

⅓ cup orange juice, or 3 tablespoons orange juice plus 2 tablespoons Cointreau

a large pinch of ground cinnamon

confectioners' sugar, sifted, for dusting

SAUCE

6 ounces semisweet chocolate, coarsely chopped

¼ cup orange juice

2 tablespoons superfine sugar

1. Grease 12 wide-top, ½-cup ovenproof demitasse coffee cups with the butter, then sprinkle them with 2 tablespoons of superfine sugar, tilting to coat them evenly. Put them on a baking sheet and set aside.

2. Put half the measured sugar and all the egg yolks into a mixing bowl and beat together for 2 minutes, using an electric handheld mixer, until thick and pale. Sift the flour over the surface, then fold it in.

3. Pour the milk into a medium, heavy saucepan, bring just to a boil, then gradually whisk it into the egg mixture until smooth. Pour the mixture back into the pan, then cook over low heat, whisking gently, until thickened and smooth.

4. Remove the soufflé mixture from the heat and whisk in the orange rind, juice, Cointreau, and cinnamon. Cover with plastic wrap and let cool.

5. Preheat the oven to 375°F. Whisk the egg whites in a large, clean mixing bowl until you have stiff, moist-looking peaks. Gradually whisk in the remaining sugar, a teaspoonful at a time. Fold the whites into the cooled soufflé mixture, then divide among the 12 dishes so that they are three-quarters full. Bake in the preheated oven for 15–20 minutes, or until the soufflés are well risen, the tops are golden, and they are almost set in the center.

6. Meanwhile, to make the sauce, put the chocolate, orange juice, and sugar in a heatproof bowl, set the bowl over a saucepan of gently simmering water, and heat until smooth and melted, stirring from time to time. Pour into a pitcher.

7. Quickly serve the soufflés on saucers, dusted with sifted confectioners' sugar, and drizzle the warm chocolate sauce over the top.

Cranberry and granola sundaes

Makes: 10
Prep: 20 minutes
Cook: 13–15 minutes

With the mix of tangy, slightly sharp cranberry compote, creamy smooth Greek yogurt, and crunchy granola, this is a great dessert or party brunch. Make up extra granola and serve in little dishes as an alternative to crisps.

a little sunflower oil, for greasing

2 tablespoons sesame seeds

2 tablespoons pumpkin seeds

¼ cup rolled oats

¼ cup slivered almonds

3 tablespoons unsalted butter

2 tablespoons honey

2 tablespoons packed light brown sugar

1 cup honey-flavored Greek yogurt

CRANBERRY COMPOTE

2 teaspoons cornstarch

⅓ cup packed light brown sugar

juice of 1 large orange

2 cups frozen cranberries

1. Preheat the oven to 350°F. Lightly brush a large baking sheet with oil.

2. Put the sesame seeds, pumpkin seeds, rolled oats, and slivered almonds into a bowl and mix together, using your fingertips. Put the butter, honey, and sugar into a heavy saucepan and heat gently until the butter has melted and the sugar dissolved. Remove from the heat and stir in the seed mixture. Transfer to the prepared baking sheet and spread into a thin, even layer. Bake in the preheated oven for 8–10 minutes, stirring halfway through cooking and moving the browned edges to the center. Let cool in the pan.

3. For the cranberry compote, put the cornstarch, sugar, and orange juice into a heavy saucepan and cook over medium heat, stirring, until smooth. Add the frozen cranberries and cook, uncovered, for 5 minutes, stirring, until they have softened and the juices have thickened. Let cool.

4. Crumble half the granola, using your fingertips, and break the rest into shards. Sprinkle a layer of the crumble into ten shot glasses, spoon a layer of yogurt over the granola, then add a layer of cranberry compote. Repeat the layers, finishing with a layer of compote, and decorate with the shards of granola. Any remaining granola shards can be served in a small separate dish.

Chocolate molten lava cakes with caramel sauce

Makes: 10
Prep: 25 minutes
Chill: 1 hour or overnight
Cook: 17–20 minutes

This restaurant favorite is surprisingly easy to make, and it can be prepared in advance and stored in the refrigerator for up to 24 hours. The secret is to bake the desserts for the precise amount of cooking time and to test one before serving them. They should be crusty on top but soft and molten in the center.

1¼ sticks unsalted butter

4 teaspoons unsweetened cocoa powder

6 ounces semisweet dark chocolate, coarsely chopped

2 eggs, plus 2 egg yolks

⅔ cup superfine sugar

3 tablespoons all-purpose flour

confectioners' sugar, sifted, for dusting

CARAMEL SAUCE

4 tablespoons unsalted butter

¼ cup packed light brown sugar

1 tablespoon honey

⅔ cup heavy cream

1. Melt 2 tablespoons of the butter in a small saucepan, then brush it over the insides of ten ½-cup ovenproof ramekins (individual ceramic dishes). Sift a little cocoa into each ramekin, then tilt to coat the bottom and sides evenly, tapping out any excess.

2. Put the chocolate and remaining stick of butter in a heatproof bowl, set the bowl over a saucepan of gently simmering water, and heat until melted, stirring from time to time.

3. Put the eggs, egg yolks, and superfine sugar into a mixing bowl and whisk together until thick and frothy and the whisk or beaters leave a trail when raised above the mixture. Sift over the flour, then gently fold it in.

4. Fold the melted chocolate mixture into the egg mixture until smooth. Pour it into the prepared ramekins, cover, and chill in the refrigerator for 1 hour, or overnight if time permits.

5. For the caramel sauce, put the butter, light brown sugar, and honey into a heavy saucepan and heat gently for 3–4 minutes, or until the butter has melted and the sugar dissolved, then boil for 1–2 minutes, stirring, until it begins to smell of caramel and thicken. Remove from the heat and stir in the cream.

6. Preheat the oven to 350°F. Take the ramekins out of the refrigerator and let them stand at room temperature for 10 minutes. Bake in the preheated oven for 10–12 minutes, or until well risen, the tops are crusty, and the centers still slightly soft. Reheat the sauce over low heat, if needed.

7. Dust the desserts with sifted confectioners' sugar. Serve with the sauce in a pitcher for guests to pour on.

Raspberry and strawberry meringues

Makes: 20
Prep: 25 minutes
Cook: 25–30 minutes

Spoil the ones you love with these beautiful little meringues. You can make them in advance and keep them in an airtight container for several days, then just make the topping when you are ready to serve them.

2 egg whites

½ cup superfine sugar

½ teaspoon cornstarch

½ teaspoon white wine vinegar

TOPPING

1¼ cups heavy cream

finely grated rind and juice of 1 lime

3 tablespoons strawberry jam or preserves

1½ cups raspberries

1½ cups hulled and sliced, small strawberries

1. Preheat the oven to 275°F. Line a large baking sheet with nonstick parchment paper.

2. Whisk the egg whites in a large, clean mixing bowl until you have stiff, moist-looking peaks. Gradually whisk in the sugar a tablespoonful at a time. Once all the sugar has been added, whisk for an additional 1–2 minutes, until the meringue is thick and glossy.

3. Mix together the cornstarch and vinegar in a small bowl until smooth, then fold it into the meringue. Spoon the mixture onto the prepared baking sheet in 20 mounds, leaving a little space between each mound. Spread it into circles 2 inches in diameter, then make a small dip in the center of each circle, using the back of a teaspoon.

4. Bake in the preheated oven for 25–30 minutes, or until the meringues are a pale golden color and can easily be lifted off the paper. If they stick to the paper, cook them for another few minutes, then retest. Let cool on the paper.

5. For the topping, pour the cream into a large mixing bowl and whisk until it forms soft swirls, then fold in the lime rind. Spoon a dollop of the cream onto the top of each meringue, then transfer to a serving plate.

6. Put the jam and lime juice in a small, heavy saucepan and place over gentle heat until the jam has just melted. Stir in the raspberries and strawberries, then let cool a little. Spoon the fruit over the meringues and serve.

Strawberry and rosé gelatins

Makes: 8
Prep: 20 minutes
Cook: 5 minutes
Chill: 4 hours

A pretty finale to any summer celebration. If you have organic roses growing in the yard, you may want to decorate the cream with tiny, pink rose petals instead of finely grated lemon rind.

1 cup hulled and sliced, small strawberries

1½ tablespoons superfine sugar

3 tablespoons water

2 teaspoons powdered gelatin

1 cup rosé wine

TOPPING

1½ tablespoons superfine sugar

2 tablespoons rosé wine

finely grated rind of 1 lemon

⅔ cup heavy cream

1. Put the strawberries and sugar into a mixing bowl and mix together, using a metal spoon.

2. Put the water in a small, heatproof bowl, then sprinkle the gelatin over the surface, making sure the powder is absorbed. Set aside for 5 minutes. Set the bowl of gelatin in a saucepan of gently simmering water and heat for about 5 minutes, stirring from time to time, until the gelatin is a clear liquid (see page 116).

3. Divide the sugar-coated strawberries among eight small champagne or liqueur glasses. Pour the wine into a small bowl or liquid measuring cup and stir in the gelatin, then pour it into the glasses. Cover and chill in the refrigerator for 4 hours, or until the gelatin has set.

4. To make the topping, put the sugar, wine, and half the lemon rind into a small bowl and stir. Pour the cream into a large mixing bowl and beat until it forms soft swirls. Add the wine mixture and beat briefly, until the cream is thick again. Spoon the lemon cream into the center of the desserts, then decorate with the remaining lemon rind.

Rippled raspberry cheesecakes

Makes: 12
Prep: 30 minutes
Cook: 5 minutes
Chill: 3 hours

8 sticks unsalted butter

1 cup crushed graham crackers

3 tablespoons water

2 teaspoons powdered gelatin

1 cup raspberries, plus 24 extra
to decorate

⅔ cup heavy cream

⅔ cup prepared custard or
vanilla pudding

¼ teaspoon vanilla extract

Silicone sheets make inverting these dainty desserts out of the cups child's play. The swirled effect is simple to create but looks really impressive.

1. Melt the butter in a saucepan, then stir in the cookie crumbs. Divide the mixture among the sections of two 6-cup silicone muffin pans; the bottom of each cup should be 1½ inches in diameter. Press over the bottom of the cups, using the back of a teaspoon, then chill in the refrigerator.

2. Put the water in a small heatproof bowl, then sprinkle the gelatin over the surface, making sure the powder is absorbed. Set aside for 5 minutes. Meanwhile, puree the 1 cup of raspberries in a blender, then press through a strainer into a bowl to remove the seeds. Set the bowl of gelatin in a saucepan of gently simmering water and heat for about 5 minutes, stirring from time to time, until the gelatin is a clear liquid (see page 116).

3. Pour the cream into a large mixing bowl and beat until it forms soft swirls. Fold in the custard or vanilla pudding and vanilla extract. Stir 1½ tablespoons of the gelatin into the raspberry puree and fold the rest into the cream mixture. Spoon the cream mixture into the muffin cups, level the surface, using the back of a teaspoon, then spoon the raspberry puree on top. Swirl together the two mixtures, using the handle of the teaspoon. Cover and chill in the refrigerator for 3 hours, or longer if time permits, until set.

4. To serve, loosen the desserts, using a blunt knife, then turn them out by pressing underneath. Decorate each dessert with two raspberries.

Lemon and blueberry duets

Makes: 10
Prep: 15 minutes
Cook: 5 minutes
Chill: 1–2 hours

1¼ cups heavy cream

½ cup superfine or granulated sugar

finely grated rind and juice of 1 lemon, plus grated rind of 1 lemon to decorate

1 teaspoon cornstarch

¼ cup water

2¾ cups blueberries

If you need a dessert in a hurry, then this is it. It takes just 20 minutes to make, then can be kept in the refrigerator to chill until you are ready to serve.

1. Put the cream and ⅓ cup sugar into a medium, heavy saucepan, then heat gently, stirring, until the sugar has dissolved. Increase the heat and bring to a boil, then cook for 1 minute, stirring.

2. Remove from the heat, add half the finely grated lemon rind and all the juice, and stir continuously for 1 minute, until the mixture begins to thicken slightly. Pour into ten shot glasses, then let cool.

3. Put the remaining sugar and finely grated lemon rind into a smaller heavy saucepan, stir in the cornstarch, then gradually mix in the water until smooth. Add half the blueberries, then place over medium heat and cook, stirring, for 3–4 minutes, until they are starting to soften and the sauce thicken.

4. Remove the compote from the heat, stir in the remaining blueberries, then let cool. Cover the glasses and blueberry compote with plastic wrap, then transfer to the refrigerator for 1–2 hours, or until set.

5. When ready to serve, stir the blueberries, then spoon them into the glasses and decorate with the grated lemon rind.

White chocolate and strawberry cheesecakes

Makes: 40
Prep: 30 minutes
Cook: 45–50 minutes
Chill: overnight

An all-American favorite, this baked cheesecake tastes even better the day after it is made.

SPONGE CAKE

4 tablespoons margarine, softened

¼ cup superfine or granulated sugar

½ cup all-purpose flour

¾ teaspoon baking powder

1 egg

CHEESECAKE

8 ounces white chocolate, coarsely chopped

2½ cups cream cheese

⅓ cup superfine or granulated sugar

1 teaspoon vanilla extract

1 cup heavy cream

4 eggs

TOPPING

1 cup crème fraîche or whipped cream

10 strawberries, hulled and quartered

2 ounces white chocolate, cut into shards, using a swivel-blade vegetable peeler

1. Preheat the oven to 350°F. Line a 12 x 8 x 2-inch loose-bottom cake pan with nonstick parchment paper, snipping diagonally into the corners, then pressing the paper into the pan so that the bottom and sides are lined.

2. Put all the sponge ingredients into a mixing bowl and beat together, using a wooden spoon, until smooth. Spoon the batter into the prepared pan and spread it into a thin layer, using a spatula. Bake in the preheated oven for 10–12 minutes, or until golden and firm to the touch. Remove from the oven and let cool. Reduce the oven temperature to 300°F.

3. For the cheesecake, put the chocolate in a heatproof bowl, set the bowl over a saucepan of gently simmering water, and heat until melted. Stir briefly and let cool. Meanwhile, put the cream cheese, sugar, and vanilla extract into a mixing bowl and beat together briefly, using an electric handheld mixer, until just smooth. Gradually beat in the cream until thick once again. Beat in the eggs, one at a time, waiting until the mixture is smooth before adding the next one. Stir in the melted chocolate.

4. Spoon the cheesecake mixture onto the sponge and spread it out so it forms an even layer. Bake in the preheated oven for 30–35 minutes, or until the edge is slightly cracked and the center still a little soft. Turn off the oven, leave the door ajar, and let it cool in the oven.

5. Cover the cheesecake and put it in the refrigerator overnight. When ready to serve, remove the cheesecake from the pan, peel off the parchment paper, and cut into 40 squares. Put these on a serving plate and top each square with a spoonful of crème fraîche. Add one-quarter of a strawberry to each square and sprinkle with white chocolate shards.

Apricot and chocolate meringues

Makes: 12
Prep: 20 minutes
Cook: 10–13 minutes

Quick and easy to make, these pretty desserts look wonderful served on a plate or platter. When apricots are out of season, try making these with halved plums.

6 apricots, halved and pitted

juice of ½ small orange

1 egg white

2 tablespoons superfine sugar

2 ounces semisweet chocolate, cut into 12 pieces

1. Preheat the oven to 350°F.

2. Arrange the apricots, cut side up, on a baking sheet. Drizzle the orange juice over the top of them. Bake in the preheated oven for 5–8 minutes.

3. Meanwhile, whisk the egg white in a large, clean mixing bowl until you have stiff, moist-looking peaks. Gradually whisk in the sugar a teaspoonful at a time. Once all the sugar has been added, whisk for an additional 1–2 minutes, until the meringue is thick and glossy.

4. Spoon the meringue into a pastry bag fitted with a medium star tip. Put a piece of chocolate in the center of each apricot.

5. If the apricots wobble, stick them to the baking sheet with a little meringue. Pipe a whirl of meringue on top of the chocolate. Bake in the preheated oven for 5 minutes, or until the meringue is tinged golden brown and just cooked. Let cool for a few minutes, then transfer to a serving plate.

Baby blueberry brûlées

Makes: 12
Prep: 20 minutes
Cook: 15 minutes
Chill: 3–4 hours

This is a girlie dessert, in health-conscious-size servings — although it will be hard to resist the temptation of second helpings!

1 cup blueberries

4 egg yolks

1 teaspoon vanilla extract

½ cup superfine or granulated sugar

1¼ cups heavy cream

1. Preheat the oven to 325°F. Put twelve ¼-cup ovenproof dishes in a large roasting pan and divide the blueberries among them.

2. Put the egg yolks, vanilla, and 3 tablespoons of sugar into a small bowl and mix together, using a fork, until smooth and creamy. Pour the cream into a small, heavy saucepan, bring to a boil, then gradually mix it into the yolks. Strain the mixture through a strainer back into the pan before pouring it back into the bowl.

3. Pour the cream mixture over the blueberries. Pour warm water into the roasting pan to come halfway up the sides of the dishes. Bake in the preheated oven for 15 minutes, or until the custard is just set, with a slight wobble in the center.

4. Let cool for 5–10 minutes, then lift the dishes out of the water and transfer to the refrigerator to chill for 3–4 hours.

5. To serve, sprinkle the remaining sugar over the dishes in an even layer, then caramelize it, using a chef's blow torch or under a broiler preheated to hot.

Berry torte

Makes: 20
Prep: 40 minutes
Cook: 25–30 minutes

Spoil the ones you love with these dainty, rich, dark chocolate cakes layered with minty strawberries and swirled with rich chocolate cream. If you don't have a heart-shape cookie cutter, use a small round one instead.

1 cup unsweetened cocoa powder

1 cup boiling water

1 stick unsalted butter, softened

2 cups packed light brown sugar

2 eggs, beaten

1⅔ cups all-purpose flour

1 teaspoon baking powder

FILLING

⅔ cup heavy cream

⅔ cup hulled and finely chopped strawberries

1 tablespoon finely chopped fresh mint

1 tablespoon superfine sugar

FROSTING

⅔ cup heavy cream

6 ounces semisweet chocolate, coarsely chopped

1. Preheat the oven to 350°F. Line a deep 10-inch square, loose-bottom cake pan with nonstick parchment paper, snipping diagonally into the corners, then pressing the paper into the pan so that the bottom and sides are lined.

2. Put the cocoa in a heatproof bowl, then gradually stir in the boiling water until you have a smooth paste. Let cool.

3. Put the butter and light brown sugar into a mixing bowl and beat together, using an electric handheld mixer until light and fluffy. Gradually beat in the eggs and a tablespoon of flour, until smooth. Sift the remaining flour and the baking powder into the bowl and fold them in, then gradually stir in the cooled cocoa mixture.

4. Pour the mixture into the prepared cake pan and spread into an even layer, using a spatula. Bake in the preheated oven for 25–30 minutes, or until risen and firm to the touch and a toothpick inserted into the center of the cake comes out clean. Let cool for 10 minutes, then transfer to a wire rack and let cool completely.

5. Remove the parchment paper and, using a 2-inch heart-shape cutter, cut out 20 cakes. Cut each cake in half horizontally.

6. For the filling, pour the cream into a large mixing bowl and beat until it forms soft swirls. Fold in the strawberries, mint, and superfine sugar, then spread the mixture over the bottom half of each cake and top with the other cake half. Put the cakes on a wire rack.

7. For the frosting, pour the cream into a small, heavy saucepan and bring just to a boil. Remove from the heat and add the chocolate. Set aside for 5 minutes, then stir until smooth and glossy. Let cool for an additional 15 minutes, until thick, then spoon onto, and spread over, the top of the cakes. Let set, then transfer to a serving plate.

Strawberry and mint ice cream cones

Makes: 24
Prep: 40 minutes
Cook: 15–20 minutes
Freeze: 6 hours plus 20 minutes

These pretty cones would be fun to serve at a family summer party. Keep a few of them in the freezer for a special last-minute treat to thrill any little girl and her friends.

CONES

4 tablespoons unsalted butter

2 egg whites

½ cup superfine or granulated sugar

a few drops of vanilla extract

½ cup all-purpose flour

ICE CREAM

½ cup superfine or granulated sugar

⅓ cup water

2 sprigs of mint

3 cups hulled and sliced strawberries (about 1 pound), plus extra to serve

1 tablespoon powdered gelatin

⅔ cup heavy cream

1. Preheat the oven to 350°F. Line three baking sheets with nonstick parchment paper. You will need eight homemade cones made out of cardboard covered with parchment paper to use as molds.

2. For the cones, melt the butter in a saucepan. Lightly whisk the egg whites in a large, clean mixing bowl until frothy but still translucent. Whisk in the sugar, then the melted butter and the vanilla. Sift in the flour, then fold it in until smooth. Drop four or five half-teaspoonfuls of the batter over one of the prepared baking sheets and spread each into a circle 2–2½ inches in diameter. Bake in the preheated oven for 3–5 minutes, or until just golden at the edges.

3. Let the baked cookies harden for a few moments, then loosen with a spatula and quickly shape into small cones around the molds. Let set for 1–2 minutes, then remove the molds. Repeat baking and shaping cones until all the batter is used, then let cool. Don't bake too many cookies at once, or they will harden before you can shape them.

4. For the ice cream, put the sugar, 2 tablespoons of water, and the mint into a medium, heavy saucepan. Heat gently, stirring from time to time, until the sugar has dissolved. Add the sliced strawberries, increase the heat slightly, and cook for 3 minutes. Discard the mint, then puree the mixture in a blender until smooth. Press the puree through a strainer into a metal loaf pan.

5. Put the remaining water in a small heatproof bowl, then sprinkle the gelatin over the surface, making sure the powder is absorbed. Set aside for 5 minutes. Set the bowl of gelatin in a saucepan of gently simmering water and heat for about 5 minutes, stirring from time to time, until the gelatin is a clear liquid (see page 116). Gently stir the gelatin into the pureed strawberry mixture, let cool, then freeze for 20 minutes.

6. Pour the cream in a large mixing bowl and beat until it forms soft swirls. Transfer the just-setting strawberry mixture to another large mixing bowl and beat for a few minutes. Fold the cream into the strawberries. Stand the cones in small cups and pipe the ice cream into them. Freeze for 6 hours or overnight. To serve, arrange the cones in a glass bowl with extra strawberries.

Triple chocolate mousses

Makes: 36
Prep: 45 minutes
Cook: 2 minutes
Chill: overnight
Freeze: 45 minutes

These fancy-looking desserts can be prepared the day before you plan to serve them, or even frozen, and are easier to slice if not fully defrosted.

4 tablespoons unsalted butter

1 tablespoon unsweetened cocoa powder

1¼ cups crushed graham crackers

milk chocolate curls, to decorate

MOUSSE

¼ cup water

4 teaspoons powdered gelatin

4 ounces semisweet chocolate, coarsely chopped

4 ounces milk chocolate, coarsely chopped

4 ounces white chocolate, coarsely chopped

1 stick unsalted butter

⅓ cup milk

6 eggs, separated

½ teaspoon vanilla extract

1½ cups heavy cream

1. Line a deep, 8-inch-square, loose-bottom cake pan with two long strips of plastic wrap, laid over each other in a cross, then press into the pan. The edges of the plastic wrap should hang over the sides of the pan.

2. Melt the butter in a small saucepan, then stir in the cocoa and cookie crumbs. Press the mixture into the pan in an even layer, then cover and chill in the refrigerator.

3. For the mousse, put the water in a small heatproof bowl, then sprinkle the gelatin over the surface, making sure the powder is absorbed. Set aside for 5 minutes. Set the bowl of gelatin in a saucepan of gently simmering water and heat for 5 minutes, stirring from time to time, until the gelatin is a clear liquid (see page 116).

4. Put each type of chopped chocolate in a different heatproof bowl, then add one-third of the butter and 2 tablespoons of milk to each bowl. Place each bowl over a saucepan of gently simmering water and heat until the chocolate has melted. Stir 2 egg yolks into each bowl, one at a time, then remove from the heat.

5. Stir 4 teaspoons of the dissolved gelatin into each bowl, then stir the vanilla into the white chocolate. Pour the cream into a fourth bowl and whisk until it forms soft swirls. Fold one-third of the cream into each of the chocolate mixtures. Whisk the egg whites in a large, clean mixing bowl until you have soft peaks, then divide them among the chocolate bowls and fold in gently.

6. Pour the dark chocolate mousse into the cookie-lined pan, spread it into an even layer, then freeze for 15 minutes. Spoon over the white chocolate layer and freeze for 30 minutes. Gently whisk the milk chocolate layer to soften, if needed, then spoon it over and chill in the refrigerator overnight, or until set.

7. To serve, lift the mousse out of the pan, pressing from the bottom. Peel off the plastic wrap. Cut the mousse into six strips, using a wet knife, then cut each strip into six small squares, wiping and wetting the knife frequently so that the layers don't become smeared. Arrange on small plates or saucers and decorate with milk chocolate curls.

Mini clementine sorbets

Makes: 10
Prep: 25 minutes
Cook: 5 minutes
Freeze: 4 hours plus overnight

If you are serving these only to adults, you might want to add a splash of Cointreau or Grand Marnier to the mixture before freezing.

10 clementines

⅓ cup granulated sugar

¼ cup water

finely grated rind and juice of 1 lemon

juice of 1 large orange

1. Cut a thin slice off the top of each clementine and set aside. Squeeze a little of the juice from each fruit into a blender. Using a teaspoon, scoop the flesh into the blender, then process to a puree.

2. Press the puree through a strainer into a large loaf pan. Put the ten clementine cups into a roasting pan and freeze.

3. Put the sugar and water into a heavy saucepan. Heat gently for 5 minutes, or until the sugar has dissolved, tilting the pan to mix them together. Increase the heat and boil rapidly, without stirring, for 1 minute. Remove from the heat, then stir in the lemon rind and juice. Pour the lemon syrup and orange juice through a strainer and onto the clementine puree, stir, then let cool.

4. Transfer the loaf pan to the freezer and freeze for 2 hours, or until the mixture is semifrozen. Break up the ice crystals, using a fork, then return to the freezer for 1 hour. Beat again with the fork, then freeze for an additional 1 hour. Beat again until it resembles colored snow.

5. Spoon the sorbet into the clementine cups, add the lids at a slanted angle, and freeze overnight. (If the sorbet has frozen too firmly, let it soften at room temperature for a few minutes, then beat with a fork.) When ready to serve, transfer the iced desserts to a plate.

Striped cranberry and amaretti creams

Makes: 10
Prep: 30 minutes
Cook: 5–8 minutes
Chill: 1 hour

An easy festive dessert that makes a great alternative to the traditional Christmas treat. Children will love to help you make the sugar stars.

⅓ cup superfine or granulated sugar

2 teaspoons cornstarch

a large pinch of ground cinnamon

a large pinch of ground ginger

½ cup water

2 cups frozen cranberries

AMARETTI CREAM

⅔ cup cream cheese

3 tablespoons superfine or granulated sugar

1 cup heavy cream

4 teaspoons orange juice or Cointreau

12 amaretti cookies, crushed

SUGAR STARS

confectioners' sugar, for dusting

6 ounces ready-to-use fondant

1. Put the sugar, cornstarch, cinnamon, and ginger into a medium, heavy saucepan, then gradually mix in the water until smooth. Add the frozen cranberries and cook gently for 5–8 minutes, stirring from time to time, until they are soft and the compote has thickened. Cover and let cool.

2. For the amaretti cream, put the cream cheese and sugar into a mixing bowl and stir, then gradually beat in the cream until smooth. Stir in the orange juice and then the cookie crumbs. Spoon the mixture into a paper or plastic disposable pastry bag. Spoon the cranberry compote into another disposable pastry bag. Snip off the tips.

3. Pipe amaretti cream into ten shot glasses until they are one-quarter full. Pipe over half the cranberry compote, then repeat the layers. Cover and chill in the refrigerator for 1 hour.

4. For the sugar stars, line a baking sheet with nonstick parchment paper. Lightly dust a work surface with confectioners' sugar. Knead the fondant lightly, then roll it out thinly. Stamp out stars of different sizes, using tiny star cutters, then transfer to the prepared baking sheet and let harden at room temperature for 1 hour, or until needed. Arrange the stars on the desserts and around the bottoms of the glasses just before you serve them.

Chocolate and caramel cups

Makes: 12
Prep: 30 minutes
Cook: 7–8 minutes
Chill: 2 hours

If you don't have any petit four liners, line the cups of a mini muffin pan with small squares of plastic wrap, spread melted chocolate over the plastic wrap, then peel it away before serving.

6 ounces semisweet chocolate, coarsely chopped

½ cup granulated sugar

¼ cup water

12 small walnut halves

2 tablespoons unsalted butter

½ cup heavy cream

1. Line a 12-cup mini muffin pan with paper petit four liners. Line a baking sheet with nonstick parchment paper.

2. Put the chocolate in a heatproof bowl, set the bowl over a saucepan of gently simmering water, and heat until melted. Put a spoonful of melted chocolate into each paper liner, then brush over the sides evenly, using a small pastry brush. Chill for 30 minutes, then brush on a second layer of chocolate, being careful around the sides so there is an even thickness. Cover and chill in the refrigerator.

3. Put the sugar and water into a small, heavy saucepan. Heat gently for 5 minutes, or until the sugar has dissolved, tilting the pan to mix them together. Increase the heat and boil rapidly without stirring for 4–5 minutes, until the caramel is deep golden (see page 116). Remove from the heat, add the walnuts, quickly coat them in the caramel, then lift them out, using two forks. Put them on the prepared baking sheet, slightly apart.

4. Add the butter to the remaining caramel, tilt the pan to mix, then gradually stir in the cream. Transfer to a bowl, let cool, then cover and chill in the refrigerator for 1½ hours, or until thick. Lift the chocolate-lined paper liners out of the pan. Spoon the caramel cream into a large pastry bag fitted with a large star tip and pipe it into the chocolate cups. Chill in the refrigerator until required. Decorate with the caramel walnuts just before serving.

Cherry and honey terrines

Makes: 30
Prep: 25 minutes
Cook: 10 minutes
Freeze: 30 minutes
Chill: 5 hours

This two-tone dessert is made by setting the gelatin mold at an angle before adding the creamy layer for an eye-catching effect.

1 (10-ounce) package frozen pitted cherries

2 tablespoons superfine or granulated sugar

¾ cup water

4 teaspoons powdered gelatin

1 cup fromage blanc or ricotta cheese

finely grated rind of 1 lemon

3 tablespoons honey

⅔ cup heavy cream

1. Put the frozen cherries, sugar, and ½ cup water into a medium, heavy saucepan, bring to a boil, then reduce the heat and simmer, uncovered, for 5 minutes, until the cherries have softened.

2. Meanwhile, put the remaining water in a small heatproof bowl, then sprinkle the gelatin over the surface, making sure the powder is absorbed. Set aside for 5 minutes. Set the bowl of gelatin in a heavy saucepan of gently simmering water and heat for 5 minutes, stirring from time to time, until the gelatin is a clear liquid (see page 116).

3. Process the cherry mixture in a blender until pureed, then pour back into the heavy saucepan. Stir in 2½ tablespoons of the gelatin mixture, then let cool.

4. Divide the cherry mixture among six ⅔-cup loaf pans, prop them up in the freezer so that the gelatin sets at an angle, then freeze for 30 minutes, or until firm.

5. Meanwhile, put the fromage blanc, lemon rind, and honey into a mixing bowl and stir together. Pour the cream into a large mixing bowl and beat until it forms soft swirls, then fold it into the fromage blanc mixture. Add the remaining gelatin mixture and stir gently, then cover and let stand at room temperature.

6. When the cherry mixture is semifrozen, spoon the fromage blanc over the top, level, then cover and chill in the refrigerator for 4 hours, or until set.

7. To invert, dip each mold in a dish of just-boiled water for 2 seconds, then lift it out of the water. Loosen the edges of each dessert with a blunt knife, then invert onto a plate, remove the pan, and clean up the edge of the dessert with a sharp knife, if needed. Return to the refrigerator for 1 hour, then slice each terrine into five and serve.

Honey and pistachio ice cream with poached figs

Makes: 10
Prep: 30–35 minutes
Cook: 10 minutes
Freeze: 1–7 hours

Refreshingly cool and summery, this Greek-inspired dessert can be made in advance and looks best served with small figs.

ICE CREAM

6 egg yolks

2 teaspoons cornstarch

⅓ cup honey

2 cups milk

1 cup Greek yogurt

2 teaspoons rose water (optional)

½ cup coarsely chopped pistachio nuts

POACHED FIGS

⅔ cup red wine

¼ cup superfine or granulated sugar

1 cinnamon stick, halved

10 small figs

1. For the ice cream, put the egg yolks, cornstarch, and honey into a large mixing bowl. Put the milk into a medium, heavy saucepan, bring to a boil, then gradually whisk it into the yolks. Strain the mixture through a strainer back into the pan and cook over low heat, stirring, until thickened and smooth. Pour the custard into a clean bowl, cover the surface with parchment paper, and let cool.

2. Whisk the yogurt and rose water, if using, into the custard. Pour the mixture into a chilled ice cream machine and churn for 15–20 minutes, until thick and creamy. Mix in the pistachio nuts and churn until stiff enough to scoop. If you don't have an ice cream machine, pour into a large nonstick loaf pan for 3–4 hours, until semifrozen. Beat in a food processor, then stir in the pistachio nuts, return to the loaf pan, and freeze for an additional 3 hours, or until firm.

3. Meanwhile, for the poached figs, put the wine, sugar, and cinnamon stick into a small, heavy saucepan and heat gently. Add the figs (they should fit snugly into the pan) and poach gently for 5 minutes. Let cool.

4. When ready to serve, take the ice cream out of the freezer and let it soften at room temperature for 5–10 minutes. Scoop into small dishes and add two fig halves and a little of the syrup. Serve immediately.

Blueberry vodka gelatins

Makes: 12
Prep: 15 minutes
Cook: 8 minutes
Chill: 4 hours

This pretty dessert can be prepared in minutes. It looks stylish served in glasses of different heights, then arranged on individual dessert plates or saucers and sprinkled with pink edible glitter.

6 ladyfingers or thin slices of store-bought pound cake

1½ cups water

1 tablespoon powdered gelatin

2 cups blueberries

⅓ cup superfine or granulated sugar

finely grated rind of 1 lemon

½ cup vodka

½ cup heavy cream

pink edible glitter, to decorate

1. Cut out 12 small circles of cake, using the top of a liqueur glass as a guide, then press each of them into the bottom of a liqueur glass.

2. Put ¼ cup of water into a small bowl, then sprinkle the gelatin over the surface, making sure the powder is absorbed. Set aside for 5 minutes.

3. Meanwhile, put the blueberries, sugar, lemon rind, and remaining 1¼ cups of water into a heavy saucepan and bring to a boil, then reduce the heat and simmer, uncovered, for 5 minutes, until the fruit has softened.

4. Take the pan off the heat, add the gelatin, and stir until it has dissolved. Add the vodka, then pour the mixture into the glasses, pressing down the cake circles with a teaspoon if they begin to float. Let cool, then cover and put the glasses on a small baking sheet. Chill in the refrigerator for 4 hours, or until set.

5. When ready to serve, spoon 2 teaspoons of the cream over the top of each dessert, then sprinkle with pink edible glitter.

Iced chocolate and peppermint mousses

Makes: 12
Prep: 40 minutes
Cook: 10 minutes
Chill: 30 minutes
Freeze: 4 hours

A classic French dessert with a twist. Because these little mousses are frozen, they can be made well in advance of your party. The drizzled chocolate decoration can be prepared the night before and kept in the refrigerator until you are ready to serve.

6 ounces semisweet chocolate, coarsely chopped

1 tablespoon unsalted butter, diced

3 eggs, separated

2 tablespoons milk

1 tablespoon superfine or granulated sugar

½ teaspoon peppermint extract

DECORATION

2 ounces semisweet chocolate, coarsely chopped

2 ounces white chocolate, coarsely chopped

a few drops of green food coloring

½ cup heavy cream

½–1 teaspoon peppermint extract

1. For the mousse, put the semisweet chocolate and butter in a heatproof bowl, set the bowl over a saucepan of gently simmering water, and heat until melted. Stir in the egg yolks, one at a time, then stir in the milk until smooth. Remove from the heat.

2. Whisk the egg whites in a large, clean mixing bowl until you have soft peaks. Gradually whisk in the sugar a teaspoonful at a time. Fold the egg whites into the melted chocolate mixture, then fold in the peppermint.

3. Spoon the mousse into 12 plastic shot glasses (if you have a funnel or large piping tip, spoon the mousse into this and pipe it into the glasses so that the sides don't get messy). Freeze for 4 hours, or overnight.

4. Meanwhile, for the decoration, line a baking sheet with nonstick parchment paper. Put the semisweet chocolate in a heatproof bowl, set the bowl over a saucepan of gently simmering water, and heat until melted. Drizzle spoonfuls of the melted chocolate over the prepared baking sheet in random squiggles, then chill in the refrigerator for 30 minutes.

5. Put the white chocolate for the decoration in a heatproof bowl, set the bowl over a saucepan of gently simmering water, and heat until melted. Drizzle half the melted white chocolate over the semisweet chocolate on the baking sheet. Stir the green food coloring into the remaining white chocolate and drizzle it over the other two layers of chocolate. Chill in the refrigerator for 30 minutes.

6. To decorate the mousses, pour the cream into a large bowl and beat until it forms soft swirls, then stir in the peppermint extract. Spoon it onto the frozen desserts, then break the drizzled chocolate into pieces and press it into the cream. Let the desserts stand at room temperature for 10 minutes, then serve.

Tropical caramel custards

Makes: 10
Prep: 25 minutes
Cook: 30–35 minutes
Chill: 4 hours

Here's a dessert with an exotic twist, with the addition of orange, lime, and mango. If you don't have small metal molds, use little foil muffin or tart liners, but make sure they're 1½ inches deep.

¾ cup granulated sugar

¾ cup water

3 tablespoons boiling water

2 eggs, plus 2 egg yolks

⅔ cup low-fat milk

1 (14-ounce) can sweetened condensed milk

finely grated rind 1 orange

finely grated rind 1 lime

½ small mango, peeled and pitted, to decorate

1. Preheat the oven to 325°F. Put ten ⅔-cup individual metal molds or dariole molds in a roasting pan.

2. Put the sugar and water into a heavy saucepan. Heat gently for 5 minutes, or until the sugar has dissolved, tilting the pan to mix them together. Increase the heat and boil rapidly without stirring for 5 minutes, until the caramel is deep golden (see page 116). Remove from the heat and add the boiling water, but stand well back because the syrup will spit. Let the syrup cool for 1 minute, or until the bubbles begin to subside, then divide it among the molds.

3. Put the eggs and egg yolks into a medium bowl, then whisk lightly with a fork.

4. Pour the milk and condensed milk into a heavy saucepan. Bring just to a boil over low heat, stirring continuously. Slowly pour this into the egg yolks, stirring all the time, then strain it back into the pan. Stir in the orange rind and half the lime rind (wrap the rest in plastic wrap and reserve).

5. Pour the custard into the molds. Pour warm water into the roasting pan to come halfway up the sides of the molds. Bake in the preheated oven for 20–25 minutes, or until the custard is set. Lift the molds out of the water, let them cool, then chill in the refrigerator for 4 hours, or overnight.

6. To serve, cut the mango into small, thin slices. Dip each mold in a dish of just-boiled water for 10 seconds, then lift it out of the water. Loosen the edges of each dessert with a blunt knife, then invert them onto a plate and remove the mold. Serve topped with the mango slices and sprinkled with the reserved lime rind.

Mini Sweets

Equipment

Heavy saucepans

Good, heavy saucepans in various sizes are crucial for working with sugar and chocolate, so they don't burn on the bottom of the pan.

Baking sheets & pans

You'll need nonstick baking sheets of various sizes, including ones that are 12 x 8 inches, 11 x 7 inches, and 8 inches square.

Heavy-duty, metal baking sheets are best because they don't buckle from the heat of the oven. Make sure you buy ones that fit in your oven.

You'll also need a loose-bottom cake pan measuring 8 inches square and another measuring 7 inches square, as well as a heavy 8-inch square baking pan and a 10-inch square baking pan for fudge.

Be sure to buy good-quality baking sheets and pans. It really is worth the extra money, because they will last a lifetime — as long as you take care of them properly.

Nonstick parchment paper

Nonstick parchment paper is invaluable for lining baking sheets and pans.

Candy thermometer

A candy thermometer is essential for cooking sugar mixtures to a particular desired temperature. It will read between 100°F and 400°F in small increments.

Make sure that the thermometer takes the temperature of the mixture in the pan and not of the bottom of the pan to get an accurate reading.

Electric mixer

The electric stand mixer is one of the most important tools for making sweets. It allows you to have your hands free while adding different ingredients or attending to other tasks as your ingredients are mixing.

Electric handheld mixer

The electric handheld mixer is crucial for beating, whipping, whisking, blending, and mixing ingredients for specific tasks, such as making macarons.

Food Processor

The food processor is one of the most useful tools in the kitchen. It's terrific for chopping and grinding nuts as well as for blending mixtures.

Measuring cups & spoons

It is essential to have a standard set of kitchen measuring cups and measuring spoons as well as a large liquid measuring cup.

Microplane graters

Invest in stainless steel, razor-sharp graters in various sizes for different tasks, such as finely grating lemon rind and making chocolate curls.

Spatula

A heat-resistant rubber spatula is invaluable for stirring mixtures as they cook.

Kitchen timer

Choose a kitchen timer that is easy to read. Always set the timer for the least amount of time called for in the recipe — you can always add more time, if needed.

Cooking techniques

Melting chocolate

Put coarsely chopped or broken chocolate in a sturdy heatproof bowl that will fit snugly over a heavy saucepan, so that no heat or steam can escape. Bring the saucepan of water to a gentle simmer, then set the bowl over it and continue simmering over low heat until the chocolate has melted. Keep the water level in the pan at no more than 1 inch deep and do not let the bottom of the bowl containing the chocolate touch the water or you may burn the chocolate. Once the chocolate has melted, use a rubber spatula to mix it until it is smooth. If you prefer to melt chocolate in a microwave, put the broken chocolate in a microwave-proof bowl and melt it on the lowest power in 30-second bursts. Stir with a rubber spatula after each burst.

Whisking eggs & egg whites

To whisk eggs to their full volume, it is best to first have them at room temperature. Use an electric stand mixer or handheld electric mixer with a bowl that is large enough for the eggs to triple in volume. Start with a medium speed and step it up to medium–high as the volume of the eggs increases in size. When whisking egg whites, it is important that the bowl is clean with no trace of grease or fat, or they won't whisk properly. Egg whites can be frozen for up to three months. To defrost, let them come to room temperature before using.

Whipping cream

Chilled cream whips best, because it holds onto the air whipped into it better. Chill the bowl and beaters if you can before whipping the cream. Start whipping on a medium speed and watch carefully, because it can easily be overwhipped and get too firm. If this happens, you can rectify it by adding another couple of tablespoons of cream and whipping gently until it becomes smooth.

Chopping nuts

Chop nuts on a cutting board using a chef's knife or pulse them using a food processor.

Strawberry ripple marshmallows

Makes: 32
Prep: 40 minutes
Cook: 20 minutes
Set: 1 hour

Light and fluffy, these pretty cubes of sweetness and light will put a smile on everyone's face. They are equally good made with raspberry extract instead of strawberry.

a little sunflower oil, for greasing

cornstarch, for dusting

confectioners' sugar, sifted, for dusting

11 sheets of sheet gelatin (approximately ¾ ounce)

1½ cups water

1 tablespoon liquid glucose

2¼ cups superfine sugar

3 egg whites

1 teaspoon strawberry extract

2 teaspoons pink food coloring

1. Lightly brush a 12 x 8-inch baking pan with oil, then lightly dust it with cornstarch and sifted confectioners' sugar.

2. Put the gelatin into a small bowl and add ½ cup of water, making sure the gelatin is absorbed. Set aside for 10 minutes.

3. Put the glucose, sugar, and remaining water into a medium, heavy saucepan. Bring to a boil, then reduce the heat and simmer for 15 minutes, or until the mixture reaches 260°F on a candy thermometer. Remove from the heat. Stir the gelatin mixture, then carefully spoon it into the pan; the syrup will bubble. Pour the syrup into a small bowl and stir.

4. Beat the egg whites in a large, clean mixing bowl until you have stiff, moist-looking peaks, then gradually beat in the hot syrup. The mixture will become shiny and start to thicken. Add the strawberry extract and beat for 5–10 minutes, until the mixture is stiff enough to hold its shape on the beaters.

5. Spoon the mixture into the prepared baking pan and smooth it, using a wet spatula. Sprinkle the food coloring over it and drag a small toothpick through it to create a marbled effect. Let set for 1 hour.

6. Loosen the marshmallow around the sides of the pan using a blunt knife, then turn out it onto a board. Cut it into 32 squares, then lightly dust with cornstarch and sifted confectioners' sugar. Place on a wire rack to dry. Serve immediately.

Apple and apricot fruit gelatins

Makes: 30
Prep: 25 minutes
Cook: 10 minutes
Set: 3-4 hours

Called "jujubes" in some countries, these fruity cubes are refreshing and delicious. You can change the fruit flavor simply by using a different fruit juice and preserves.

2 cups apple juice

3 tablespoons powdered gelatin

2 cups superfine sugar

1½ cups apricot preserves

1. Put half the apple juice into a mixing bowl, then sprinkle the gelatin over the surface, making sure the powder is absorbed (see page 116). Set aside for 10 minutes.

2. Meanwhile, put the remaining apple juice and half the sugar into a heavy saucepan. Boil, stirring, for 5–6 minutes, or until the sugar has dissolved. Whisk in the preserves, then return to a boil and cook for 3–4 minutes, until the mixture is thick and syrupy. Whisk the gelatin into the syrup until it dissolves.

3. Pour the mixture through a fine-mesh strainer into a bowl. Transfer it to a 10 x 7-inch nonstick cake pan. Chill in the refrigerator for 3–4 hours, or until set.

4. Spread the remaining sugar over a large baking sheet. Cut the fruit gelatin into 30 squares and remove from the pan using a spatula. Toss in the sugar to coat just before serving. Serve or store in an airtight container in a cool, dry place for up to five days.

Raspberry coconut ice

Makes: 20
Prep: 30 minutes
Set: 3 hours

A no-cook sweet treat that is perfect to make with the kids. This is a wonderful gift when wrapped in cellophane bags or little gift boxes.

a little sunflower oil, for greasing

2½ cups confectioners' sugar, sifted, plus extra if needed

4½ cups dry unsweetened flaked coconut

1 (14-ounce) can sweetened condensed milk

1 teaspoon vanilla extract

½ cup raspberries

½ teaspoon pink food coloring

1 teaspoon raspberry extract

1. Lightly brush an 8-inch square baking pan with oil. Line the bottom with nonstick parchment paper.

2. Put half the sifted confectioners' sugar and half the coconut into one mixing bowl and put the other half into a second bowl. Stir the contents of each bowl, then make a well in the center.

3. Add half the condensed milk and half the vanilla to each of the coconut mixtures and stir. Press one of the mixtures into the prepared baking pan and level, using a spatula.

4. Put the raspberries into a blender and process to a puree. Push this through a strainer into a bowl to remove the seeds. Add the puree, food coloring, and raspberry extract to the remaining coconut mixture. Add more sifted confectioners' sugar if the mixture is too wet.

5. Spread the pink coconut ice over the white coconut layer, cover, then chill in the refrigerator for 3 hours, or until set.

6. Lift the coconut ice out of the pan, peel off the paper, and cut into 20 squares. Store in an airtight container in a cool, dry place for up to five days.

Mini toffee apples

Makes: 12
Prep: 25 minutes
Cook: 12–15 minutes

3 large red apples

juice of 1 lemon

½ cup superfine or granulated sugar

¾ cup water

1 tablespoon unsalted butter

a few drops of red food coloring

Nothing beats the crunch of a homemade toffee apple during a fall evening. Dunking the hot toffee into iced water ensures a crisp shell.

1. Put a bowl of iced water in the refrigerator. Using a melon scoop, scoop out 12 balls from the apples, making sure each ball has some red skin on it. Push a small toothpick into each ball through the red skin. Squeeze the lemon juice over the apple balls to prevent them from discoloring; set aside.

2. Put the sugar, water, and butter into a medium, heavy saucepan. Heat gently until the sugar has dissolved, tilting the pan to mix the ingredients together. Increase the heat and boil rapidly for 12–15 minutes, or until the mixture reaches 320°F on a candy thermometer and is deep golden. Turn off the heat, stir in the food coloring, and let the bubbles subside.

3. Remove the bowl of iced water from the refrigerator. Working as quickly as possible, dip the apples into the toffee, one at a time, rotating them a few times to get an even coating, then drop them into the iced water for 30 seconds. Serve immediately.

Pistachio and apricot nougat

Makes: 16
Prep: 30 minutes
Cook: 15 minutes
Set: 8–10 hours

A confection made from boiled honey and sugar syrup mixed with beaten egg white, nuts, and dried fruit. It is associated with the French town of Montélimar, where it has been made since the eighteenth century. Enjoy it as an after dinner candy with coffee, crumble it over ice cream, or use it in desserts.

edible rice paper

1¼ cups superfine sugar

½ cup liquid glucose

⅓ cup honey

2 tablespoons water

a pinch of salt

1 egg white

½ teaspoon vanilla extract

4 tablespoons unsalted butter, softened and diced

⅓ cup coarsely chopped pistachio nuts

⅓ cup finely chopped dried apricots

1. Line a 7-inch square baking pan with plastic wrap, leaving an overhang. Line the bottom with edible rice paper.

2. Put the sugar, glucose, honey, water, and salt into a heavy saucepan. Heat gently until the sugar has dissolved, tilting the pan to mix the ingredients together. Increase the heat and boil for 8 minutes, or until the mixture reaches 250°F on a candy thermometer.

3. Put the egg white into a freestanding mixer, or use a handheld mixer, and beat until firm. Gradually pour in one-quarter of the hot syrup in a thin stream while still beating the egg. Continue beating for 5 minutes, until the mixture is stiff enough to hold its shape on the beaters.

4. Put the pan containing the remaining syrup over gentle heat for 2 minutes, or until the mixture reaches 290°F on a candy thermometer. Gradually pour the syrup over the egg mixture while beating.

5. Add the vanilla and butter and beat for an additional 5 minutes. Add the pistachios and apricots and stir.

6. Pour the mixture into the prepared baking pan and level, using a spatula. Cover with edible rice paper and chill in the refrigerator for 8–10 hours, or until fairly firm.

7. Lift the nougat out of the pan and cut into 16 squares. Serve or store in an airtight container in the refrigerator for up to five days.

Peanut butter and chocolate candy balls

Makes: 36
Prep: 25 minutes
Cook: 5 minutes
Set: 4–6 hours

This recipe uses semisweet chocolate to coat the peanut candy balls, but, if you prefer, you can use milk or white chocolate, or a mixture of the three.

1 cup smooth peanut butter

4 tablespoons unsalted butter

¾ cup crisp rice cereal

1⅔ cups confectioners' sugar

8 ounces semisweet chocolate, coarsely chopped

1. Line two baking sheets with nonstick parchment paper. Melt together the peanut butter and butter in a heavy saucepan.

2. Put the rice cereal and confectioners' sugar into a large mixing bowl. Pour in the melted butter mixture, then stir. When cool enough to handle, using the palms of your hands, roll the mixture into 1-inch balls, then put them on the prepared baking sheets and chill in the refrigerator for 3–4 hours, or until firm.

3. Put the chocolate in a heatproof bowl, set the bowl over a saucepan of gently simmering water, and heat until melted.

4. Using two teaspoons, dip the balls into the chocolate, one by one, making sure they are covered completely, then lift them out and return them to the baking sheets. Chill in the refrigerator for 1–2 hours, or until set. Serve or store in an airtight container in the refrigerator for up to five days.

Sea-salted pecan candies

Makes: 12
Prep: 15 minutes
Cook: 10–15 minutes
Set: 10 minutes

You can replace the pecans with walnuts, whole peeled almonds, or cashew nuts, if you prefer.

½ cup pecans

1½ cups superfine sugar

¾ cup water

2 teaspoons sea salt

1. Preheat the oven to 325°F. Put the pecans on a baking sheet and toast them in the preheated oven for 3–4 minutes, or until golden, shaking them halfway through. Divide the nuts among the cups of a 12-cup silicone mini muffin pan.

2. Put the sugar and water into a heavy saucepan. Heat gently, tilting the pan to mix together the ingredients, until the sugar has dissolved and the mixture reaches an even light brown color. Continue cooking until it is a slightly deeper brown, watching it carefully so it doesn't burn. Sprinkle with the sea salt and transfer to a liquid measuring cup or pitcher for easy pouring.

3. Quickly pour the mixture into the muffin cups. Let cool for 10 minutes, until the candies set and harden. Turn the candies out of the cups. Store in an airtight container in a cool, dry place for up to five days.

Toffee popcorn

Makes: 200 g/7 oz
Prep: 15 minutes
Cook: 5–10 minutes

2 tablespoons unsalted butter

½ cup popping corn

TOFFEE COATING

3 tablespoons unsalted butter

¼ cup packed dark brown sugar

2 tablespoons light corn syrup

This popcorn is fun to make as a treat for children's birthday parties. For adults, sprinkle over a little cayenne pepper to get a sweet and spicy kick.

1. Melt the butter in a large, heavy saucepan. Add the popping corn and swirl the pan to coat the corn evenly.

2. Cover the pan with a tight-fitting lid, reduce the heat to low, and let the corn start popping. Shake the pan a couple of times to move the unpopped pieces to the bottom. As soon as the popping stops, take the pan off the heat and let stand, covered.

3. For the toffee coating, melt the butter in a medium, heavy saucepan. Add the sugar and syrup and cook over high heat, stirring, for 1–2 minutes, or until the sugar has dissolved.

4. Pour the toffee coating over the popped corn, replace the lid on the pan, and shake well. Let cool slightly, then serve immediately.

Honeycomb brittle

Makes: approx 20
Prep: 15 minutes
Cook: 10–15 minutes
Set: 5 minutes

Known as hokey-pokey in Australia, this light and crunchy brittle is perfect broken into bite-size pieces or crushed over ice cream.

a little sunflower oil, for greasing

1 cup superfine sugar

½ cup light corn syrup

1 stick unsalted butter, diced

2 teaspoons baking soda

1. Lightly brush an 8-inch square baking pan with oil.

2. Put the sugar, syrup, and butter into a large, heavy saucepan. Heat gently until the sugar has dissolved, tilting the pan to mix the ingredients together. Increase the heat and boil rapidly for 4–5 minutes, or until the mixture turns a light golden color.

3. Add the baking soda and stir for a few seconds; be careful because the mixture will expand and bubble.

4. Pour the mixture into the prepared baking pan. Let cool for 5 minutes, or until set. Break the brittle into shards. Store in an airtight container in a cool, dry place for up to two weeks.

Sesame, marshmallow, and cranberry squares

Makes: 20
Prep: 15 minutes
Cook: 20 minutes

These are best baked in advance. They make a great afternoon treat or lunch box filler.

$1^2/_3$ cup rolled oats

$^1/_3$ cup sesame seeds

3 tablespoons packed light brown sugar

$^2/_3$ cup miniature marshmallows

$^1/_2$ cup dried cranberries

$^1/_2$ cup honey

$^1/_3$ cup sunflower oil, plus extra for greasing

a few drops of vanilla extract

1. Preheat the oven to 325°F. Lightly brush an 11 x 7-inch baking pan with oil. Line the bottom with nonstick parchment paper.

2. Put the oats, sesame seeds, sugar, marshmallows, and cranberries into a mixing bowl and stir. Make a well in the center, add the honey, oil, and vanilla extract, then stir again.

3. Press the mixture into the prepared baking pan and level, using a metal spoon. Bake in the preheated oven for 20 minutes, or until golden and bubbling.

4. Let cool in the pan for 10 minutes, then cut into small squares. Let cool completely before turning out of the pan. Store in an airtight container in a cool, dry place for up to two days.

Cashew nut brittle

Makes: approx 20
Prep: 15 minutes
Cook: 25–30 minutes

This is a wonderful, buttery brittle that is easy to make and wows everyone! You could use roasted peanuts instead of cashew nuts, if you prefer.

1¼ cups roasted, salted cashew nuts

1¾ cups superfine sugar

¼ teaspoon cream of tartar

1 cup water

1 tablespoon unsalted butter

1. Line an 8-inch square baking pan with nonstick parchment paper.

2. Spread the cashew nuts in the baking pan in a thin, even layer.

3. Put the sugar, cream of tartar, and water into a heavy saucepan. Bring to a gentle boil over medium heat, stirring all the time.

4. Reduce the heat to low and simmer for 20–25 minutes without stirring, until the mixture reaches 290°F on a candy thermometer. Stir in the butter, then carefully drizzle the caramel over the nuts. Let cool completely.

5. Break the brittle into shards. Serve or store in an airtight container in a cool, dry place for up to two days.

Vanilla fudge

Makes: 16
Prep: 15 minutes
Cook: 12–15 minutes
Set: 1 hour

Just five simple ingredients and you can make the creamiest vanilla fudge ever. A guaranteed hit! Be careful when you stir the fudge, because the mixture gets very hot.

a little sunflower oil, for greasing

2¼ cups superfine or granulated sugar

6 tablespoons unsalted butter

⅔ cup whole milk

⅔ cup evaporated milk

2 teaspoons vanilla extract

1. Lightly brush an 8-inch square baking pan with oil. Line the bottom with nonstick parchment paper.

2. Put the sugar, butter, milk, and evaporated milk into a heavy saucepan. Heat gently, stirring, until the sugar has dissolved.

3. Increase the heat and boil for 12–15 minutes, or until the mixture reaches 240°F on a candy thermometer (if you don't have a candy thermometer, spoon a little of the syrup into some iced water; it will form a soft ball when it is ready). As the temperature rises, stir the fudge occasionally so the sugar doesn't stick and burn.

4. Remove the pan from the heat, add the vanilla, and beat, using a wooden spoon, until thickened.

5. Pour the mixture into the prepared baking pan and smooth the surface, using a spatula. Let cool for 1 hour, or until set.

6. Lift the fudge out of the pan, peel off the paper, and cut into small squares. Store in an airtight container in a cool, dry place for up to two weeks.

Indulgent whiskey fudge

Makes: 16
Prep: 15 minutes
Cook: 12–15 minutes
Set 2–3 hours

If you are a chocolate and whiskey lover, this is the perfect edible treat. You can use a good brandy instead of whiskey, if you prefer.

a little sunflower oil, for greasing

1 cup packed brown sugar

1 stick unsalted butter, diced

1 (14-ounce) can sweetened condensed milk

2 tablespoons glucose syrup

¼ cup walnut pieces

6 ounces semisweet chocolate, coarsely chopped

¼ cup whiskey

1. Lightly brush an 8-inch square baking pan with oil. Line it with nonstick parchment paper, snipping diagonally into the corners, then pressing the paper into the pan so that the bottom and sides are lined.

2. Put the sugar, butter, condensed milk, and glucose into a heavy saucepan. Heat gently, stirring, until the sugar has dissolved. Increase the heat and boil for 12–15 minutes, or until the mixture reaches 240°F on a candy thermometer (if you don't have a candy thermometer, spoon a little syrup into some iced water; it will form a soft ball when it is ready). As the temperature rises, stir the fudge occasionally so the sugar doesn't burn.

3. Meanwhile, preheat the broiler to medium-hot. Put the walnuts in a baking sheet and toast them under the broiler for 2–3 minutes, or until browned. Coarsely chop them.

4. Remove the fudge from the heat. Add the chocolate and whiskey and stir together until the chocolate has melted and the mixture is smooth.

5. Pour the mixture into the prepared baking pan, smooth the surface, using a spatula, and sprinkle the walnuts over it. Let cool for 1 hour. Cover with plastic wrap, then chill in the refrigerator for 1–2 hours, or until firm. Lift the fudge out of the pan, peel off the paper, and cut into 16 squares. Store in an airtight container in a cool, dry place for up to two weeks.

Chocolate Pretzel fudge squares

Makes: 16
Prep: 15 minutes
Cook: 8–10 minutes
Set: 2–3 hours

These are so easy to make. The salty pretzels counteract the rich sweetness of the chocolate and condensed milk.

1 (7-ounce) package mini pretzels

a little sunflower oil, for greasing

2 tablespoons unsalted butter, diced

1¾ cups milk chocolate chips

1 (14-ounce) can sweetened condensed milk

1 teaspoon vanilla extract

1. Coarsely chop one-third of the pretzels.

2. Lightly brush a 10-inch square baking pan with oil. Line it with nonstick parchment paper, snipping diagonally into the corners, then pressing the paper into the pan so that the bottom and sides are lined and there is a 2-inch overhang on all sides.

3. Put the butter, chocolate chips, condensed milk, and vanilla in a heatproof bowl, set the bowl over a saucepan of gently simmering water, and heat, stirring occasionally, for 8–10 minutes, or until the chocolate has just melted and the mixture is smooth and warm but not hot. Remove from the heat and stir in the chopped pretzels.

4. Pour the mixture into the prepared pan, smooth the surface, using a spatula, and push in the whole pretzels. Let cool for 1 hour. Cover with plastic wrap, then chill in the refrigerator for 1–2 hours, or until firm.

5. Lift the fudge out of the pan, peel off the paper, and cut it into 16 squares. Store in an airtight container in a cool, dry place for up to two weeks.

Chocolate-coated candied orange rind

Makes: 36
Prep: 55 minutes
Cook: 1 hour
Set: 2–4 hours

Strips of candied orange rind dipped in dark chocolate make an elegant gift. Alternatively, serve them with coffee after dinner.

3 large navel oranges

1 cup granulated sugar

8 ounces semisweet chocolate, coarsely chopped

1. Using a sharp knife, cut the rind off the oranges, then remove the white pith from the rind. Slice the rind into thirty-six 2½ x ½-inch strips, discarding any you don't need.

2. Bring a small saucepan of water to a boil, then add the orange rind and simmer for 10 minutes. Drain, then rinse under cold running water. Pour more water into the pan and bring it to a boil again, then return the rind to the pan and simmer for an additional 10 minutes. Repeat this process one more time.

3. Put the sugar and 1 cup of water into a heavy saucepan. Bring to a boil and simmer gently, stirring, for 5 minutes, or until the sugar has dissolved and the mixture has reduced a little in volume. Add the orange rind and continue simmering for 15 minutes. Transfer the candied peel to a wire rack and let cool for 1–2 hours or overnight.

4. Line a baking sheet with nonstick parchment paper. Put the chocolate in a heatproof bowl, set the bowl over a saucepan of gently simmering water, and heat until melted.

5. Dip one-third of the length of each candied orange strip in the chocolate and place it on the prepared baking sheet. Let cool for 1–2 hours, or until set. Store in an airtight container in a cool, dry place for up to five days.

Salted caramel and chocolate bites

Makes: 20
Prep: 30 minutes
Cook: 35–40 minutes

Sea salt and caramel is a classic combination, and here it is enhanced by the addition of walnuts.

a little sunflower oil, for greasing

8 ounces semisweet chocolate, coarsely chopped

1¼ sticks unsalted butter

2 eggs

¾ cup packed light brown sugar

½ cup all-purpose flour

1 teaspoon baking powder

½ cup coarsely chopped walnuts

⅓ cup dulce de leche (caramel sauce)

1 tablespoon sea salt

1. Preheat the oven to 325°F. Lightly brush an 8-inch square baking pan with oil. Line it with nonstick parchment paper, snipping diagonally into the corners, then pressing the paper into the pan so that the bottom and sides are lined.

2. Put 2 ounces of the chocolate and all the butter in a heatproof bowl, set the bowl over a saucepan of gently simmering water, and heat until melted, stirring from time to time.

3. Put the eggs and sugar into a mixing bowl, then sift in the flour and baking powder. Stir in the melted chocolate mixture and whisk together until blended. Add the walnuts and remaining chocolate and stir together. Pour the mixture into the prepared baking pan and smooth the surface, using a spatula.

4. Put the dulce de leche into a small mixing bowl and beat, then swirl it through the chocolate mixture using a fork. Sprinkle with the sea salt and bake in the preheated oven for 30–35 minutes, or until the cake begins to shrink slightly from the sides of the pan. Let cool for 1 hour.

5. Lift the cake out of the pan, peel off the paper, and cut it into 20 squares. Store in an airtight container in a cool, dry place for up to two days.

White and dark chocolate-dipped strawberries

Makes: 24
Prep: 10 minutes
Cook: 3-4 minutes
Set: 1 hour

Chocolate always makes a sweet mouthful special, and in this fun, party treat it is paired with delicious strawberries. Prepare it several hours before you plan to serve it, if you prefer.

4 ounces semisweet chocolate, coarsely chopped

4 ounces white chocolate, coarsely chopped

24 large strawberries

1. Line a baking sheet with nonstick parchment paper. Put the semisweet chocolate and white chocolate into two separate heatproof bowls, set the bowls over two saucepans of gently simmering water, and heat until melted.

2. Dip the pointed end of each strawberry into one of the melted chocolates and transfer it to the prepared baking sheet. Let cool for 1 hour, or until set.

3. Put each strawberry in a liqueur glass or on a plate and serve immediately.

Mini cranberry and ginger florentines

Makes: 48
Prep: 30 minutes
Cook: 15–20 minutes
Set: 2 hours

These crispy and chewy bites are an Italian classic and make a marvelous present.

⅓ cup packed brown sugar

¼ cup honey

1 stick unsalted butter, plus extra for greasing

¾ cup dry unsweetened flaked coconut

¾ cup slivered almonds

1 tablespoon finely chopped candied peel

1 tablespoon finely chopped preserved ginger

⅔ cup dried cranberries

½ cup all-purpose flour, plus extra for dusting

8 ounces semisweet chocolate, coarsely chopped

1. Preheat the oven to 350°F. Using butter, lightly grease four 12-cup miniature muffin pans (the bottom of each cup should be ¾ inch in diameter), then lightly dust them with flour.

2. Put the sugar, honey, and butter into a heavy saucepan. Heat gently, stirring, until the sugar has dissolved, tilting the pan to mix together the ingredients. Stir in the coconut, almonds, candied peel, preserved ginger, cranberries, and flour.

3. Put small teaspoons of the batter into the prepared muffin pans. Bake in the preheated oven for 10–12 minutes, or until golden brown. Let cool in the pans for 1 hour. Using a spatula, transfer to a wire rack until firm.

4. Meanwhile, put the chocolate in a heatproof bowl, set the bowl over a saucepan of gently simmering water, and heat until melted.

5. Dip each florentine into the melted chocolate so the bottom is covered. Place on a wire rack, chocolate side up, and let set for 1 hour. Store in an airtight container in a cool, dry place for up to two days.

Nutty peppermint bark

Makes: approx 25
Prep: · 20 minutes
Cook: 3–4 minutes
Set: 30 minutes

Kids and adults alike will love this treat. If you can't get hold of peppermint candy canes, substitute them with any mint candy.

7 ounces red-and-white striped peppermint candy canes, broken into pieces

1 pound white chocolate, coarsely chopped

1 cup chopped mixed nuts

1. Line a 12 x 8-inch baking sheet with nonstick parchment paper.

2. Put the broken candy into a large plastic food bag and seal tightly. Using a rolling pin, bash the bag until the candy is crushed into small pieces.

3. Put the chocolate in a heatproof bowl, set the bowl over a saucepan of gently simmering water, and heat until melted. Remove from the heat and stir in three-quarters of the candy.

4. Pour the mixture into the prepared baking sheet, smooth the surface, using a spatula, and sprinkle over the chopped nuts and remaining candy. Press down slightly to make sure they stick. Cover with plastic wrap and chill in the refrigerator for 30 minutes, or until firm.

5. Break the peppermint bark into small, uneven pieces. Store in an airtight container in a cool, dry place for up to two weeks.

Peppermint creams

Makes: 25
Prep: 30 minutes
Set: 25 hours

The pretty and tasty peppermint cream is an old-fashioned favorite. It's a refreshing choice for an after dinner treat.

1 extra-large egg white

2½ cups confectioners' sugar, sifted, plus extra for dipping if needed

a few drops of peppermint extract

a few drops of green food coloring

4 ounces semisweet chocolate, coarsely chopped

1. Line a baking sheet with nonstick parchment paper.

2. Lightly whisk the egg white in a large, clean mixing bowl until it is frothy but still translucent.

3. Add the sifted confectioners' sugar to the egg white and stir, using a wooden spoon, until the mixture is stiff. Knead in the peppermint extract and food coloring.

4. Using the palms of your hands, roll the mixture into walnut-size balls and place them on the prepared baking sheet. Use a fork to flatten them; if it sticks to them, dip it in confectioners' sugar before pressing. Put the creams in the refrigerator to set for 24 hours.

5. Put the chocolate in a heatproof bowl, set the bowl over a saucepan of gently simmering water, and heat until melted. Dip the creams halfway in the chocolate and return to the baking sheet for 1 hour, or until set. Store in an airtight container in the refrigerator for up to five days.

Chocolate and amaretto truffles

Makes: 12
Prep: 30 minutes
Soak: 6–8 hours
Cook: 5–10 minutes
Set: 1–2 hours

These delectable morsels are so easy to make and look really glamorous! Use any liqueur instead of the amaretto, if you prefer.

¼ cup amaretto liqueur

⅓ cup golden raisins

4 ounces semisweet chocolate, coarsely chopped

2 tablespoons heavy cream

2½ ounces of store-bought chocolate cake or brownie, crumbled

1 cup hazelnuts

¼ cup chocolate sprinkles, to decorate

1. Put the amaretto and golden raisins into a small mixing bowl, cover, and let soak for 6–8 hours. Line a baking sheet with nonstick parchment paper.

2. Transfer the amaretto mixture to a food processor and process until pureed.

3. Put the chocolate and cream in a heatproof bowl, set the bowl over a saucepan of gently simmering water, and heat until melted. Remove from the heat, add the amaretto puree and chocolate cake, and stir well.

4. When cool enough to handle, using the palms of your hands, roll the mixture into truffle-size balls and place on the prepared baking sheet.

5. Preheat the broiler to medium. Put the hazelnuts on a second baking sheet and toast them under the broiler for 2–3 minutes, or until browned, shaking them halfway through. Finely chop them.

6. Spread the chocolate sprinkles onto one plate and the hazelnuts onto another. Roll half the truffles in the chocolate and half in the hazelnuts. Return to the baking sheet, cover with nonstick parchment paper, and chill in the refrigerator for 1–2 hours, or until firm. Store in an airtight container in the refrigerator for up to five days.

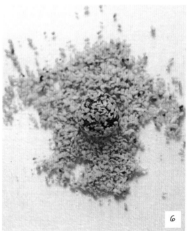

Lemon and white chocolate creams

Makes: 12
Prep: 40 minutes
Cook: 5–10 minutes
Set: 13–18 hours

For an Asian twist on these decadent truffles, add a large pinch each of ground cardamom seeds and star anise to the cream-and-chocolate mixture.

10 ounces white chocolate, coarsely chopped

2 tablespoons heavy cream

finely grated rind of 1 lemon

2 tablespoons limoncello

4 tablespoons unsalted butter, softened and diced

3 tablespoons finely chopped pistachio nuts

1. Put 4 ounces of the chocolate and all the cream in a heatproof bowl, set the bowl over a saucepan of gently simmering water, and heat until melted.

2. Remove from the heat, add the lemon rind, limoncello, and butter, and beat for 3–4 minutes, or until thickened. Transfer to an airtight container and chill in the refrigerator for 6–8 hours, or until firm.

3. Line a baking sheet with nonstick parchment paper. Scoop teaspoonfuls of the mixture and, using the palms of your hands, roll them into truffle-size balls. Place the balls on the prepared baking sheet, cover with plastic wrap, and freeze for 6–8 hours.

4. Put the remaining chocolate in a heatproof bowl, set the bowl over a saucepan of gently simmering water, and heat until melted. Using two forks, dip each truffle into the chocolate to coat evenly. Return them to the prepared baking sheet, sprinkle the pistachios over them, and chill in the refrigerator for 1–2 hours, or until firm. Store in an airtight container in the refrigerator for up to five days.

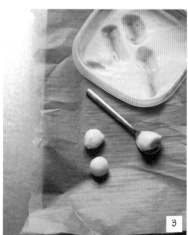

Espresso truffles

Makes: 12
Prep: 40 minutes
Cook: 5–10 minutes
Set: 13–18 hours

For a twist on these coffee truffles, simply replace the coffee with Irish cream liqueur or any orange-flavored liqueur.

10 ounces semisweet chocolate, coarsely chopped

2 tablespoons heavy cream

1 tablespoon strong espresso coffee, cooled

2 tablespoons coffee liqueur

4 tablespoons unsalted butter, softened and diced

edible gold leaf, to decorate (optional)

1. Put 4 ounces of the chocolate and all the cream in a heatproof bowl, set the bowl over a saucepan of gently simmering water, and heat until melted.

2. Remove from the heat, add the espresso, coffee liqueur, and butter, and beat for 3–4 minutes, or until thickened. Transfer to an airtight container and chill in the refrigerator for 6–8 hours, or until firm.

3. Line a baking sheet with nonstick parchment paper. Scoop teaspoonfuls of the mixture and, using the palms of your hands, roll them into truffle-size balls. Place the balls on the prepared baking sheet, cover with plastic wrap, and freeze for 6–8 hours.

4. Put the remaining chocolate in a heatproof bowl, set the bowl over a saucepan of gently simmering water, and heat until melted. Using two forks, dip each truffle into the chocolate to coat evenly. Return them to the prepared baking sheet and chill in the refrigerator for 1–2 hours, or until firm. Top each truffle with edible gold leaf to decorate, if desired. Store in an airtight container in the refrigerator for up to five days.

Chili and cardamom chocolate thins

Makes: 40
Prep: 30 minutes
Cook: 5–10 minutes
Set: 1–2 hours

These simple treats are perfect for kids to make. They're ideal for putting into a pretty box and giving as a present, too.

CHILI DARK CHOCOLATE THINS

8 ounces semisweet chocolate, coarsely chopped

a large pinch of hot chili powder

edible glitter, to decorate

CARDAMOM WHITE CHOCOLATE THINS

8 ounces white chocolate, coarsely chopped

½ teaspoon cardamom seeds, crushed

3 tablespoons finely chopped pistachio nuts, plus extra to decorate

edible glitter, to decorate

1. Line four baking sheets with nonstick parchment paper.

2. For the chili dark chocolate thins, put the semisweet chocolate in a heatproof bowl, set the bowl over a saucepan of gently simmering water, and heat until melted. Remove from the heat and stir in the chili powder.

3. Drop teaspoons of the chocolate mixture onto two of the prepared baking sheets. Sprinkle with a little edible glitter before the chocolate sets. Let set in a cool place, but not in the refrigerator, for 1–2 hours.

4. For the cardamom white chocolate thins, put the white chocolate in a heatproof bowl, set the bowl over a saucepan of gently simmering water, and heat until melted. Remove from the heat and stir in the cardamom and pistachios.

5. Drop teaspoonfuls of the white chocolate mixture onto the remaining two prepared baking sheets. Sprinkle the remaining chopped pistachios and a little edible glitter over them before the chocolate sets. Let set in a cool place, but not in the refrigerator, for 1–2 hours. Store in an airtight container in a cool, dry place for up to five days.

Iced citrus marzipan thins

Makes: 30
Prep: 25 minutes
Set: overnight

Originally from Aix-en-Provence in France, these easy-to-make after dinner treats are full of citrus and almond goodness.

2 cups ground almonds
(almond meal)

1 cup superfine sugar

1 extra-large egg

a few drops of citrus extract

finely grated rind of ½ orange

FOR THE ICING

1⅔ cups confectioners' sugar,
sifted, plus extra for dusting

juice of 1 lemon

1. Line an 8-inch square baking pan with nonstick parchment paper, snipping diagonally into the corners, then pressing the paper into the pan so that the bottom and sides are lined. Lightly dust a work surface with confectioners' sugar.

2. Put the almonds and superfine sugar into a mixing bowl and stir. Add the egg, citrus extract, and orange rind and mix, using your hands, to form a stiff paste.

3. Knead the marzipan briefly on the prepared work surface, then press it into the bottom of the prepared pan, using the back of a spoon, until even and smooth. Let set for 1 hour.

4. For the icing, put the sifted confectioners' sugar and lemon juice into a mixing bowl and stir until smooth, then spread evenly over the marzipan. Cover and let stand in a cool place, but not the refrigerator, to dry overnight.

5. Cut the iced marzipan into bite-size shapes of your choice, using a candy or cookie cutter. Store in an airtight container in the refrigerator for up to two days.

Index